Devoted To My Beloved Parents

<u>Disclaimer</u>

This Question Bank is the intellectual work of the author, resemblance of any question with any of the previous year NET question(s) or with any other question bank's question(s) will merely be a coincidence.

<u>Preface</u>

This Question Bank is especially compiled for the National Eligibility Test(NET), State Eligibility Test(SET), Junior Research Fellow(JRF) aspirants and for those who want to clear Bachelor of Library & Information Science(B.L.I.Sc.), Master of Library & Information Science(M.L.I.Sc.), Master of Philosophy(LIS), Doctor of Philosophy(LIS) entrance exams of various universities or colleges.

This Question Bank has been divided into eight units as per the latest syllabus of Library & Information Science.

In this Question Bank the answers of the questions of each unit are given at the end of that unit.

The questions framed in this question bank are more informative instead of merely expressive to prepare the readers in a better way so that they would be able to grasp more and at the same time to increase the chances to crack the various competitive exams in the field of Library & Information Science (LIS).

Table of Contents

History & Fundamentals of Library & Information Science

1. The British library movement includes the following major reports.
   Arrange them in the correct chronological order:

(i)Mc Colvin Report   (ii)Kenyen Report
(iii)Adams Report   (iv)Select Committee Report

Codes:
(A)(iv)(iii)(i)(ii)   (B)(i)(iii)(ii)(iv)
(C)(iv)(iii)(ii)(i)   (D)(i)(ii)(iv)(iii)

2. Arrange the following Librarians of National Library in the
   chronological order of their service:

(i)D.R.Kalia   (ii)Y.M.Mulay
(iii)B.S.Kesavan   (iv)K.M.Asadullah

Codes:
(A)(iv)(iii)(ii)(i)   (B)(ii)(i)(iii)(iv)
(C)(i)(iii)(ii)(iv)   (D)(iii)(i)(iv)(ii)

3. Arrange the following Library Associations according to their year of
   establishment:

(i)ILA   (ii)IASLIC
(iii)IFLA   (iv)ALA

Codes:
(A)(iii)(iv)(ii)(i)   (B)(ii)(iii)(i)(iv)
(C)(iv)(iii)(i)(ii)   (D)(i)(iii)(ii)(iv)

4. Arrange the following committees/commissions according to their
   year of formation:

(i)National Library Review Committee
(ii)Library Advisory Commission
(iii)Sinha Committee(Public Libraries)
(iv)Working group on libraries (Planning Commission)

Codes:

(A)(i)(iv)(iii)(ii)   (B)(iii)(ii)(iv)(i)
(C)(ii)(iii)(i)(iv)   (D)(iv)(ii)(i)(iii)

5. Skill Development Programme for librarians of public libraries in
   India was initiated by:

(A)MHRD   (B)RRRLF
(C)ILA   (D)DLS Govt.of W.Bengal

6. Books of unknown or doubtful authorship are known as:

(A)Blue Books   (B)Apocryphal Books
(C)Apograph   (D)Incunabula

7. Books printed before 1501 A.D. are known as:

(A)Incunabula   (B)Apograph
(C)Blue Books   (D)Early Text

8. A copy or transcript of a manuscript is known as:

(A)Monograph   (B)Blue Book
(C)Apocryph   (D)Apograph

9. A specialized work of writing on a single subject or on a particular
   aspect of a subject often by a single author is known as:

(A)Apocrypha   (B)Monograph
(C)Early Text   (D)Incunabula

10. A written work dealing formally and systematically with a subject is
    known as:

(A)Treatise   (B)Binary work
(C)Incunabula   (D)Apocrypha

11. Who was the first Librarian of Imperial Library (Calcutta)?
(A)Harinath De   (B)John MacFarlane
(C)B.S.Kesavan   (D)Dr.S.R.Ranganathan

12. The concept of "Ask Library Anything" was the initiative of:

(A)ASLIB   (B)ALA
(C)SLA   (D)ILA

13. Arrange the following books of Dr.S.R.Ranganathan, according to
    their year of publication:

(A)CC (colon classification)
(B)Elements of library classification
(C)Philosophy of library classification
(D)Prolegomena to library classification

Codes:
(i)(c)(d)(b)(a)   (ii)(b)(c)(d)(a)
(iii)(d)(c)(b)(a)   (iv)(a)(d)(b)(c)

14. Arrange these public library acts in the chronological order of their
    enactment:

(i)Tamil Nadu   (ii)Andhra Pradesh
(iii)Karnataka   (iv)Maharashtra

Codes:
(A)(ii)(i)(iv)(iii)   (B)(i)(ii)(iii)(iv)
(C)(iv)(ii)(i)(iii)   (D)(iii)(i)(ii)(iv)

15. Arrange these public library acts in the chronological order of their
    enactment:

(i)West Bengal   (ii)Manipur
(iii)Haryana   (iv)Kerala

Codes:
(A)(i)(ii)(iii)(iv)   (B)(ii)(iii)(iv)(i)
(C)(i)(ii)(iv)(iii)   (D)(iv)(i)(ii)(iii)

16. Arrange these public library acts in the chronological order of their
    enactment:

(i)Mizoram   (ii)Odisha
(iii)Goa   (iv)Gujrat

Codes:
(A)(i)(ii)(iii)(iv)   (B)(iv)(iii)(ii)(i)
(C)(iii)(iv)(i)(ii)   (D)(i)(iii)(ii)(iv)

17. Arrange these public library acts in the chronological order of their enactment:

(i)Uttar Pradesh   (ii)Rajhasthan
(iii)Uttranchal   (iv)Lakshadweep

Codes:
(A)(iii)(ii)(i)(iv)   (B)(i)(iv)(ii)(iii)
(C)(ii)(iii)(i)(ii)   (D)(iv)(ii)(iii)(i)

18. Arrange these public library acts in the chronological order of their enactment:

(i)Chhattisgarh   (ii)Bihar
(iii)Lakshadweep   (iv)Arunachal Pradesh

Codes:
(A)(iii)(ii)(i)(iv)   (B)(i)(ii)(iii)(iv)
(C)(ii)(iii)(i)(iv)   (D)(iv)(ii)(iii)(i)

19. Arrange the following library associations according to their year of emergence:

(i)CILIP   (ii)ALA
(iii)SLA   (iv)ASLIB

Codes:
(A)(ii)(iii)(iv)(i)   (B)(i)(ii)(iii)(iv)
(C)(iv)(ii)(iii)(i)   (D)(iii)(iv)(i)(ii)

20. Match the following:

List-I	List-II
(a)Library advisory committee	(i)1962
(b)Review committee	(ii)1963
(c)DRTC	(iii)1957
(d)Sarada Ranganathan Endowment	(iv)1961

Codes:
```
     (a)(b)(c)(d)
(A)(iii)(iv)(i)(ii)
(B)(i)(ii)(iii)(iv)
(C)(iv)(ii)(i)(iii)
(D)(iv)(iii)(ii)(i)
```

21. "Sarada Ranganathan Endowment for Library Science" is situated at:

(A)New Delhi   (B)West Bengal
(C)South India   (D)Bangalore

22. The use of CD-ROMs in libraries is related to which of the following Law?

(A)Third Law   (B)Forth Law
(C)Fifth Law   (D)Second Law

23. Where the first M.Phil programme in Library and Information Science was started in India?

(A)University of Madras   (B)University of Delhi
(C)University of Mysore   (D)University of Bombay

24. Corollary to Second Law of Library Science is:

(A)Books for all   (B)Free Books Service
(C)Free Library Service   (D)Books every where

25. The significance of the year 2011 for LIS education in India is:

(A)Golden Jubilee year   (B)Platinum Jubilee year
(C)Diamond Jubilee year   (D)Centenary year

26. "RRRLF" comes under:

(A)Ministry of Human Resource Development
(B)Ministry of Information & Broadcasting
(C)Ministry of Culture
(D)Ministry of Science & Technology

27. Which libraries are functioning as depository libraries?

(i)Delhi Public Library   (ii)Connemara Public Library
(iii)British Council Library   (iv)Central Reference Library

Codes:
(A)(i)(iii)&(iv) are correct   (B)(i)&(iii) are correct
(C)(i)&(ii) are correct   (D)(ii)&(iii) are correct

28. Arrange the following associations according to their year of
    establishment:

(i)IASLIC   (ii)ASLIB
(iii)ALA   (iv)SLA

Codes:
(A)(iv)(ii)(iii)(i)   (B)(ii)(iii)(iv)(i)
(C)(iii)(iv)(ii)(i)   (D)(i)(iv)(ii)(iii)

29. Arrange the following according to their year of establishment:

(i)NIC   (ii)DESIDOC
(iii)NISCAIR   (iv)NASSDOC

Codes:
(A)(i)(iii)(ii)(iv)   (B)(iii)(i)(iv)(ii)
(C)(iv)(i)(iii)(ii)   (D)(ii)(iv)(i)(iii)

30. Which one of the following is not a virtual library?

(A)Without walls
(B)With distributed physical locations
(C)Providing integrated and unified remote access to geographically
    distributed collections
(D)Which does not exist in reality

31. The national convention regularly organized by DELNET is known
    as:

(A)CALIBER   (B)ICDL
(C)NACLIN   (D)DELNETCON

32. The principle which states that "Between two or more possible
    alternatives bearing on a particular phenomenon, the one leading
    to overall economy is to be preferred" is known as:

(A)Law of Osmosis   (B)Law of Parsimony
(C)Law of Impartiality   (D)Law of Symmetry

33. The principle which states that "When switching from one scheme
    of classification to another, the library first reclassify the most
    used material" is:

(A)Law of Impartiality   (B)Law of Parsimony
(C)Law of Osmosis   (D)Law of Symmetry

34. Match the following:

List-I	List-II
(a)Konnemara public library	(i)Patna
(b)Khudabaksh oriental public library	(ii)Calcutta
(c)Asiatic society library	(iii)Chennai
(d)National library of India	(iv)Mumbai

Codes:

   (a)(b)(c)(d)

(A)(iv)(ii)(i)(iii)

(B)(iv)(i)(ii)(iii)

(C)(iii)(ii)(i)(iv)

(D)(iii)(i)(iv)(ii)

35. The Five Laws of Library Science were enunciated by Ranganathan in the year:

(A)1930

(B)1928

(C)1927

(D)1931

36. "Location" is an implication of which Law of Library Science?

(A)Second Law

(B)Third Law

(C)Fourth Law

(D)First Law

37. "Loan policy, Days of operation & Library furniture" is the implications of which Law of Library Science?

(A)Fourth Law

(B)First Law

(C)Fifth Law

(D)Third Law

38. "Book for all" is corollary to which Law of library science?

(A)Second Law

(B)First Law

(C)Third Law

(D)Fourth Law

39. "Collection development" is an implication of which Law of library science?

(A)Third Law

(B)Second Law

(C)Forth Law

(D)First Law

40. "Choice of books, Choice of staff, Duty of staff, Reference service & Resource sharing" is the implications of which Law of library science?

(A)Fifth Law　　　　　　(B)Fourth Law
(C)Second Law　　　　　(D)First Law

41. "List of books" is an implication of which Law of library science?

(A)Third Law　　　　　　(B)Second Law
(C)Forth Law　　　　　　(D)First Law

42. "Display of new books, Exhibition & Catalogue" is the implications of which Law of library science?

(A)Fifth Law　　　　　　(B)Third Law
(C)Second Law　　　　　(D)First Law

43. "Open access" is an implication of which Law of library science?

(A)Third Law　　　　　　(B)Second Law
(C)Forth Law　　　　　　(D)First Law

44. "Charging system, Classification & Cataloguing" is the implications of which Law of library science?

(A)Fourth Law　　　　　(B)Third Law
(C)Second Law　　　　　(D)First Law

45. "Library building" is an implication of which Law of library science?

(A)Third Law　　　　　　(B)Second Law
(C)Forth Law　　　　　　(D)Fifth Law

46. "Collection development, Staff strength, User strength, Reader services & weeding out" is the implications of which Law of library science?

(A)Fifth Law　　　　　　(B)Third Law
(C)Second Law　　　　　(D)First Law

47. "ILA" stands for:

(A)International library association
(B)Indian library association

(C)Intellectual library association
(D)Indian literacy association

48. "ILA" was established in the year:

(A)1933   (B)1934
(C)1932   (D)1930

49. The first "All India Library Conference" was held at:

(A)Delhi   (B)Culcutta
(C)Mumbai   (D)Chennai

50. "J.Saha, A.K.Mukherjee & G.B.Ghosh" founded which library
    association?

(A)ILA   (B)ALA
(C)DLA   (D)IASLIC

51. "IASLIC" was found at:

(A)Culcutta   (B)Delhi
(C)Mumbai   (D)Chennai

52. "IASLIC" was found in the year:

(A)1954   (B)1955
(C)1953   (D)1952

53. Dr.S.R.Ranganathan was a teacher of which subject?

(A)Law   (B)Mathematics
(C)Psychology   (D)English

54. In which year, Ranganathan was appointed as the 'Librarian' of
Madras university?

(A)1924 A.D.   (B)1920 A.D.
(C)1923 A.D.   (D)1922 A.D.

55. "Education" is an example of which kind of subject?

(A) Micro-subject   (B) Compound subject
(C) Simple subject   (D) Macro-subject

56. "Medicine, Physics & Psychology" is an example of which kind of subject?

(A) Simple subject   (B) Compound subject
(C) Micro-subject   (D) Macro-subject

57. "Child Medicine" is an example of which kind of subject?

(A) Simple subject   (B) Compound subject
(C) Micro-subject   (D) Macro-subject

58. "Child Education & Child Medicine" is an example of which kind subject?

(A) Simple subject   (B) Macro-subject
(C) Micro-subject   (D) Compound subject

59. The subject with "Greater Intension" and "Smaller Extension" is called:

(A) Complex subject   (B) Simple subject
(C) Macro-subject   (D) Micro-subject

60. The subject has "More Number of Characteristics" is called:

(A) Micro-subject   (B) Complex subject
(C) Simple subject   (D) Macro-subject

61. "An article in a periodical" is an example of which kind of subject?

(A) Simple subject   (B) Compound subject
(C) Micro-subject   (D) Macro-subject

62. The subject with "Greater Extension" and "Smaller Intension" is
    called:

(A)Complex subject   (B)Simple subject
(C)Macro-subject   (D)Micro-subject

63. The subject has "More Number of Entities" is called:

(A)Micro-subject   (B)Compound subject
(C)Simple subject   (D)Macro-subject

64. "Social sciences, History, Geography, Pure sciences & Applied
    sciences" is an example of which kind of subject?

(A)Simple subject   (B)Macro-subject
(C)Micro-subject   (D)Compound subject

65. The subject "Research Methodology" is an example of which mode
    of subject formation?

(A)Distillation   (B)Fusion
(C)Fission   (D)Lamination

66. The subject "Biology" is an example of which mode of subject
    formation?

(A)Distillation   (B)Fusion
(C)Fission   (D)Lamination

67. The subject "Biochemistry" is an example of which mode of subject
    formation?

(A)Distillation   (B)Fusion
(C)Fission   (D)Lamination

68. The subject "Gandhiana" is an example of which mode of subject
    formation?

(A)Distillation   (B)Fusion
(C)Fission   (D)Cluster

69. The subject "Child Psychology" is an example of which mode of
    subject formation?

(A)Lamination   (B)Fusion
(C)Fission   (D)Cluster

70. ILA became the member of IFLA in the year:

(A)1958   (B)1957
(C)1959   (D)1960

UNIT-I
Answers

1(A)	2(A)	3(C)	4(A)	5(B)	6(B)	7(A)	8(D)	9(B)
10(A)	11(B)	12(B)	13(iv)	14(B)	15(A)	16(D)	17(A)	18(A)
19(A)	20(A)	21(D)	22(C)	23(B)	24(A)	25(D)	26(C)	27(C)
28(C)	29(D)	30(B)	31(C)	32(B)	33(C)	34(D)	35(B)	36(D)
37(B)	38(A)	39(B)	40(C)	41(A)	42(B)	43(C)	44(A)	45(D)
46(A)	47(B)	48(A)	49(B)	50(D)	51(A)	52(B)	53(B)	54(A)
55(C)	56(A)	57(B)	58(D)	59(D)	60(A)	61(C)	62(C)	63(D)
64(B)	65(A)	66(C)	67(B)	68(D)	69(A)	70(B)		

1. Among the following which one is not a canon given by
   Dr.S.R.Ranganathan:

(A)Canon of Consistence   (B)Canon of Context
(C)Canon of Comprehensiveness   (D)Canon of Currency

2. Match the following:

List-I	List-II
(a)DDC	(i)1933
(b)CC	(ii)1876
(c)RIC	(iii)1905
(d)UDC	(iv)1961

Codes:
       (a)(b)(c)(d)
(A)(ii)(i)(iv)(iii)
(B)(i)(ii)(iii)(iv)
(C)(ii)(iii)(i)(iv)
(D)(iv)(i)(ii)(iii)

3. The term "Literary Warrant" for book classification was introduced
   by:

(A)W.Hulme   (B)W.C.B.Sayers
(C)H.E.Bliss   (D)J.D.Brown

4. Which notation is used to increase the capacity of an "Array"?

(A)Empty digit   (B)Emptying digit
(C)Indicator digit   (D)Speciator

Codes:
(i)A and B are correct   (ii)C and D are correct
(iii)A,B and C are correct   (iv)A,B and D are correct

5. In which scheme of classification, special auxiliaries denote locally recurrent characteristics:

(A)UDC   (B)DDC
(C)BC   (D)CC

6. The DDC number "540"is for the subject:

(A)Law   (B)Psychology
(B)Social Science   (D)Education

7. Which principles are corollary to Wall-Picture principle?

(i)Cow-Calf principle   (ii)Principle of later-in-time
(iii)Whole-organ principle   (iv)All of the above

Codes:
(A)(i) and (iii) is correct   (B)(i) and (ii) is correct
(C)(ii) and (iii) is correct   (D)(iii) and (i) is correct

8. When two or more basic subjects having same relational approach form a specific subject, the relation is termed as:

(A)Speciater relation   (B)Co-ordinate relation
(C)Phase relation   (D)Hierarchical relation

9. "Biotechnology" is formed as a result of:

(A)Fusion   (B)Lamination
(C)Fission   (D)Agglomeration

10. The order of significance of "Thing, Material and Action" among various components of a compound subject was expanded by:

(A)J.Kaiser   (B)E. J.Coates
(C)J.R.Sharp   (D)J.E.L.Farradane

11. Arrange the following according to their year of origin:

(i)Broad System of Ordering
(ii)Classification in Online Systems

(iii)Automated Keyword Classification
(iv)Classification Research Group

Codes:
(A)(iv)(iii)(i)(ii)   (B)(i)(ii)(iv)(iii)
(C)(iii)(i)(ii)(iv)   (D)(ii)(iv)(iii)(ii)

12. Research in automatic classification for information retrieval of term or cluster of terms is called:

(A)Evaluation theory   (B)Theory of clumps
(C)Time binding theory   (D)Dynamic theory

13. Which among the following is a "Freely-faceted & Analytico-synthetic" scheme of classification?

(A)CC   (B)DDC
(C)UDC   (D)LC

14. "Melvil Dewey" was born on:

(A)1852 A.D.   (B)1851 A.D.
(C)1853 A.D.   (D)1854 A.D.

15. "Melvil Dewey" was born at:

(A)Hague, Paris   (B)Adams centre, New York
(C)London, UK   (D)Delhi, India

16. Melvil Dewey, graduated from 'Amherst College' in the year:

(A)1874 A.D.   (B)1873 A.D.
(C)1872 A.D.   (D)1871 A.D.

17. "Colon classification" is based on which principle?

(A)Cow-calf principle   (B)Meccano principle
(C)Wall-picture principle   (D)Non of the above

18. In which year the first edition of "Colon classification" was published?

(A)1933 A.D.   (B)1932 A.D.
(C)1931 A.D.   (D)1930 A.D.

19. Classification number helps a user to locate a book:

(A)On shelf   (B)In catalogue
(C)Both   (D)Non of the above

20. "Canon of Reticence" belongs to:

(A)Idea plane   (B)Notational plane
(C)Verbal plane   (D)Non of the above

21. Colon classification has the provision of how many kinds of phase relations?

(A)3   (B)5
(C)4   (D)7

22. In colon classification 6th edition, anteriorising common isolates are divided into:

(A)5   (B)2
(C)3   (D)7

23.Total number of tables in DDC 22nd edition is:

(A)6   (B)5
(C)7   (D)4

24. "Canon of characteristics" is a part of:

(A)Verbal plane   (B)Idea plane
(C)Notational plane   (D)Structural plane

25. Which is the oldest classification scheme in the following?

(A)DDC   (B)UDC
(C)CC   (D)LC

26. "Canon of Recall value" was added in the year:

(A)1970   (B)1972
(C)1969   (D)1968

27. In DDC a dot (.)is used after three digits for:

(A)Giving aid to memory
(B)Making the class numbers as decimal numbers
(C)maintaining a tradition
(D)Non of the above

28. The use of subject device in CC is in accordance with:

(A)Alphabetical mnemonics   (B)Scheduled mnemonics
(C)Systemmatic mnemonics   (D)Seminal mnemonics

29. Which among the following fundamental categories is considered
      as most concrete:

(A)Personality   (B)Matter
(C)Energy   (D)Time

30. The first edition of DDC consisted of:

(A)44 pages   (B)144 pages
(C)224 pages   (D)04 pages

31. Match the following:

List-I	List-II
(a)C.A. Cutter	(i)Bibliographic classification
(b)J.D. Brown	(ii)Expensive classification
(c)S.R.	(iii)Subject

Ranganathan	classification
(d)H.E.	(iv)Colon
Bliss	classification

Codes:

   (a)(b)(c)(d)

(A)(i)(ii)(iii)(iv)

(B)(ii)(iii)(iv)(i)

(C)(iv)(ii)(i)(iii)

(D)(iii)(ii)(iv)(i)

32. The classification scheme which uses two or more species of digits, the notation of such scheme is known as:

(A)Mixed notation   (B)Pure notation

(C)Compound notation   (D)Complex notation

33. The "Principle of Literary Warrant" deals with the:

(A)Forms of literature

(B)Inclusion of subjects in a classification scheme

(C)Leadership style

(D)Non of the above

34. The 23rd edition of DDC was published in the year:

(A)2011   (B)2010

(C)2012   (D)2013

35. In "Medical Science" the main class of CC, the isolate 'Treatment' is categorized as:

(A)Personality isolate   (B)Matter isolate

(C)Time isolate   (D)Energy isolate

36. In DDC 19th edition '-03' will be used for:

(A)Dictionary   (B)Biography

(C)Miscellany   (D)Serials

37. A class number is assigned to a document on the basis of:

(A)Author's thinking
(B)Thought content of the document
(C)Preface of the document
(D)Acknowledgement of the document

38. Which among the following is a "Fully Enumerative scheme" of
    library classification?

(A)DDC   (B)CC
(C)UDC   (D)LCC

39. Which among the following is a "Faced scheme" of library
    classification?

(A)DDC   (B)CC
(C)UDC   (D)LCC

40. The 1st edition of DDC was published in the year:

(A)1876   (B)1877
(C)1878   (D)1879

41. The 7th edition of "Colon Classification" was published in the year:

(A)1976   (B)1977
(C)1878   (D)1987

42. "Expensive Scheme of library classification" was developed by:

(A)Melvil Dewey   (B)Charles M.E.Cutter
(C)S.R.Ranganathan   (D)H.E.Bliss

43. The 1st edition of "Expensive Classification" was published in the
    year:

(A)1891   (B)1892
(C)1893   (D)1890

44. The 1st edition of "Library of Congress Classification" was published
in the year:

(A)1901   (B)1902
(C)1903   (D)1900

45. "Paul Otlet & Henry La Fontaine" developed which scheme of
library classification?

(A)DDC   (B)CC
(C)LCC   (D)UDC

46. "UDC" stands for:

(A)Universal Decimal Classification
(B)Library of Congress Classification
(C)Dewey Decimal Classification
(D)Colon Classification

47. In which year UDC was developed?

(A)1904   (B)1905
(C)1906   (D)1900

48. "Bibliographic Classification" was developed by:

(A)Ranganathan   (B)Paul Otlet
(C)H.E.Bliss   (D)Melvil Dewey

49. "Bibliographic Classification" was developed in the year:

(A)1935   (B)1930
(C)1936   (D)1931

50. "Interpolation & Extrapolation" is related to:

(A)Cataloguing   (B)Classification
(C)Accessioning   (D)Trade literature

51. The 2nd edition of Colon Classification was published in the year:

(A)1939   (B)1938
(C)1937   (D)1936

52. The 3rd edition of Colon Classification was published in the year:

(A)1951   (B)1952
(C)1950   (D)1953

53. The 4th edition of Colon Classification was published in the year:

(A)1951   (B)1952
(C)1950   (D)1953

54. The 5th edition of Colon Classification was published in the year:

(A)1951   (B)1952
(C)1957   (D)1953

55. The 6th edition of Colon Classification was published in the year:

(A)1960   (B)1952
(C)1961   (D)1963

56. "Octave Device" is related to:

(A)Extrapolation   (B)Interpolation
(C)Empty digit   (D)Empting digit

57. Ranganathan has suggested how many "Fundamental categories" in colon classification?

(A)3   (B)6
(C)4   (D)5

58. There are how many tables in DDC 19th edition?

(A)7   (B)6
(C)8   (D)5

59. "Table 2" in DDC 19th edition is related to:

(A)Area   (B)Language
(C)Literature   (D)Social science

60. In DDC 19th edition "Table 7" is related to:

(A)Persons   (B)Ethnic group
(C)Language   (D)Area

61. "APUPA" is closely related to:

(A)Classification   (B)Rectification
(C)Shelving   (D)Cataloguing

62. DDC 23rd edition was published in the year:

(A)2011   (B)2010
(C)2012   (D)2009

63. Who is the editor in chief of DDC 19th edition?

(A)John P.Comaromi   (B)Benjamin A.Custer
(C)Winton E.Matthews   (D)John S.Mitchell

64. Who is the editor in chief of DDC 20th edition?

(A)John P.Comaromi   (B)Benjamin A.Custer
(C)Winton E.Matthews   (D)John S.Mitchell

65. Who is the editor in chief of DDC 21st edition?

(A)John P.Comaromi   (B)Benjamin A.Custer
(C)Winton E.Matthews   (D)John S.Mitchell

66. Who is the editor in chief of DDC 22nd edition?

(A)John P.Comaromi   (B)Benjamin A.Custer
(C)Winton E.Matthews   (D)John S.Mitchell

67. Who is the editor in chief of DDC 23rd edition?

(A)John P.Comaromi   (B)Benjamin A.Custer
(C)Winton E.Matthews   (D)John S.Mitchell

68. In colon classification "Part-I" is:

(A)Rules   (B)Schedule
(C)Index   (D)Classics

69. In colon classification "Part-II" is:

(A)Rules   (B)Schedule
(C)Index   (D)Classics

70. In DDC "200" is for:

(A)Religion   (B)Philosophy
(C)Literature   (D)Language

Answers

1(C)	2(A)	3(A)	4(i)	5(A)	6(A)	7(A)	8(C)	9(A)
10(B)	11(A)	12(B)	13(A)	14(B)	15(B)	16(A)	17(B)	18(A)
19(C)	20(C)	21(B)	22(C)	23(A)	24(B)	25(A)	26(C)	27(A)
28(B)	29(D)	30(A)	31(B)	32(A)	33(B)	34(A)	35(D)	36(A)
37(B)	38(D)	39(C)	40(A)	41(D)	42(B)	43(A)	44(A)	45(D)
46(A)	47(B)	48(C)	49(A)	50(B)	51(A)	52(C)	53(B)	54(C)
55(A)	56(B)	57(D)	58(A)	59(A)	60(A)	61(C)	62(A)	63(B)
64(A)	65(C)	66(D)	67(D)	68(A)	69(B)	70(A)		

Library Cataloguing

1. Bibliographic coupling was first advocated by:

(A)Dr.S.R.Ranganathan   (B)B.K.Sen
(C)M.M.Kessler   (D)S.C.Bradford

2. The complete bibliographic details in "MARC" are available in:

(A)Control fields   (B)Variable fields
(C)Record directing   (D)Leader

3. Arrange the following indexing systems in the order of their origin:

(i)POPSI   (ii)PRECIS
(iii)Chain Indexing   (iv)KWIC

Codes:
(A)(iv)(i)(ii)(iii)   (B)(i)(ii)(iv)(iii)
(C)(ii)(i)(iii)(iv)   (D)(iii)(ii)(i)(iv)

4. The primary distinction between RDA and AACR is:

(A)Structural   (B)Combinational
(C)Relational   (D)Non-structural

5. "Nina E. Browne" is associated with:

(A)Cataloguing   (B)Charging & Discharging
(C)Issue & Return   (D)Classification

6. Which Section of AACR-II (R), deals with serial publications?

(A)Part-A, Section-3   (B)Part-B, Section-3
(C)Part-A, Section-12   (D)Part-B, Section-12

7. The concept of 'Stopword' list is relevant in the context of:
(A)Uniform Indexing   (B)Citation Indexing
(C)Chain Indexing   (D)Keyword Indexing

8. A version of KWIC augmented with author/name is called:

(A)WADEX   (B)KWOC
(C)KWAC   (D)KWIC

9. "Prevention of Cholera in India" generates following index terms
   according to modified 'Chain Indexing', arrange them in correct
   order:

(i)India   (ii)Cholera
(iii)Disease   (iv)Treatment
(v) Medicine

Codes:
(A)(iii)(iv)(i)(ii)(v)   (B)(ii)(i)(iii)(iv)(v)
(C)(iv)(iii)(ii)(v)(i)   (D)(i)(iii)(iv)(v)(ii)

10. Read the following example and indicate the name of the indexing
    system used:

   "Remuneration of teachers in French universities"

The index headings are set as the following two lines:

*France*Universities *Teachers *Remuneration
*Universities *France *Teachers *Remuneration

(A)Chain procedure   (B)POPSI
(C)PRECIS   (D)KWIC

11. As specified by AACR-II (R), the source of information for machine
    readable data file is

(A)Internal user label   (B)Title page
(C)Colophone   (D)Title frame

12. How do we render the name 'Bernardo Augustine De Voto'?

(A)Voto, Bernardo Augustine De
(B)De Voto, Augustine, Bernardo
(C)Bernardo Augustine, De Voto

(D)De Voto, Bernardo Augustine

13. Union catalogue refers to the catalogue of:

(A)Students' union   (B)Trade union
(C)Soviet union   (D)A group of libraries

14. The tool used to locate Books in a library is:

(A)Magzine   (B)Newspaper
(C)Library catalogue   (D)Publisher's list

15. The publisher of "Sear's list of subject headings" is:

(A)OCLC   (B)ALA
(C)H.W.Wilson   (D)R.R.Bowker

16. Sear's list of subject headings is used for:

(A)Generating author indexes
(B)Generating title indexes
(C)Generating book Indexes
(D)Generating subject indexes

17. Symbol used in AACR-II to join two parallel titles is:

(A)Stroke sign(/)   (B)Hyphen sign(-)
(C)Equal sign(=)   (D)Semi colon(;)

18. Chain procedure was introduced in the year:

(A)1937   (B)1938
(C)1940   (D)1935

19. GMD stands for:

(A)General Material Description
(B)General Material Designation
(C)General Manuscript Designation
(D)General Management Database

20. MARC 21 was developed in the year:

(A)1997   (B)1990
(C)1999   (D)1995

21. In a list of subject heading SA is used for representing:

(A)See also   (B)See and
(C)See as   (D)See all

22. Which of the following is not a main role operator of PRECIS:

(A)Key system   (B)Location
(C)Personality   (D)Agent

23. Pre-coordinate indexing system is used in:

(A)Chain indexing   (B)Uniterm indexing
(C)Citation indexing   (D)Peek a system

24. Recall and precision ratio is usually used in the evaluation of:

(A)Reference service   (B)Information retrieval
(C)Bibliographic service   (D)DDS

25. "Worldcat" is a product of:

(A)Library of congress   (B)INFLIBNET
(C)British Library   (D)OCLC

26. The Newark charging system was introduced in the year:

(A)1896   (B)1900
(C)1929   (D)1940

27. The "three card system" was introduced by:

(A)S.R.Ranganathan   (B)Melvil Dewey
(C)J.H.Shera   (D)Taylor

28. Which among the following is a "Referral tool"?

(A)Worldcat   (B)Union catalogue
(C)Agricat   (D)Indcat

29. "Indcat" is a product of:

(A)Library of congress   (B)INFLIBNET
(C)British Library   (D)OCLC

30. "AACR" stand for:

(A)Anglo American Cataloguing Rules
(B)Anglo Association Classified Rules
(C)American Association Compressed Regulations
(D)Anglo Administered Catalogue Regulations

31. "CCC" stand for:

(A)Classified Catalogue Code
(B)Classified Catalyst Code
(C)Classification cataloguing Code
(D)Classo-Classified Code

32. The word "Catalogue" is originated from which language?

(A)Latin   (B)Greek
(C)Pushto   (D)English

33. The "Rules for Dictionary catalogue" was published in the year:

(A)1879   (B)1878
(C)1877   (D)1876

34. "Rules for Dictionary catalogue" was published by:

(A)Paul Otlet   (B)Ranganathan
(C)C.A.Cutter   (D)Melvil Dewey

35. "Loose Sheaf Form" is a form of:

(A)Library catalogue   (B)Bibliography
(C)Trade catalogue   (D)Accession Register

36. "AACR-I" was published in the year:

(A)1969   (B)1968
(C)1967   (D)1966

37. "Canon of Prepotence" is related to:

(A)Cataloguing   (B)Classification
(C)Accessioning   (D)Trade literature

38. "Canons of Cataloguing" were given by:

(A)S.R.Ranganathan   (B)H.E.Bliss
(C)Melvil Dewey   (D)M.E.Cutter

39. "Law of Impartiality" is related to:

(A)Cataloguing   (B)Classification
(C)Accessioning   (D)Trade literature

40. "AACR-II" was published in the year:

(A)1981   (B)1980
(C)1978   (D)1979

41. "KWIC" stands for:

(A)Keyword in context   (B) Keyword in content
(C)Kiwi in context   (D)Kiwi in content

42. "KWOC" stands for:

(A)Keyword out of context   (B)Keyword out of content
(C)Kiwi out of context   (D)Kiwi out in content

43. "KWAC" stands for:

(A)Keyword augmented in context
(B)Keyword associated in context
(C)Keyword association in content
(D)Keyword associated in content

44. "Unit Card System" is closely related to:

(A)APUPA   (B)Cataloguing
(C)Classification   (D)Shelving

45. In Classified Catalogue Code, CIE stands for:

(A)Classified index entry   (B)Class index entity
(C)Class index entry   (D)Classed information entry

46. In Sear's List of Subject Headings, RT stands for:

(A)See also   (B)Related Text
(C)Relational term   (D)Related Term

47. "MARC" stands for:
(A)Machine Readable Catalogue
(B)Machine Ready Catalog
(C)Mechanical Ready Catalog
(D)Machine Ready Cataloguing

48. "OPAC" stands for:
(A)Online Public Access Catalogue
(B)Open Public Access Catalogue
(C)Online Private Access Catalogue
(D)Open Private Access Catalogue

49. "Anthoni Pannizi" was the chief librarian of:
(A)Hague Museum   (B)Indian Museum
(C)American Museum   (D)British Museum

50. In ISBD(S), (S) is used for:
(A)Sacred Books   (B)Serials
(C)Sections   (D)Services

Answers

1(C) 2(B) 3(D) 4(A) 5(B) 6(C) 7(D) 8(A) 9(C)

10(C) 11(A) 12(A) 13(D) 14(C) 15(C) 16(D) 17(C) 18(B)

19(A) 20(C) 21(A) 22(C) 23(A) 24(B) 25(D) 26(B) 27(A)

28(B) 29(B) 30(A) 31(A) 32(B) 33(D) 34(C) 35(A) 36(C)

37(A) 38(A) 39(A) 40(C) 41(A) 42(A) 43(A) 44(B) 45(C)

46(D) 47(A) 48(A) 49(D) 50(B)

Information Sources & Services in Library & Information Science

1. Which source will you consult to get the information on controversies about the venue for Tata 'Nano'?

(A)Asian Recorder   (B)India: A reference annual
(C)Whitekar's Almanac   (D)New Encyclopedia Britannica

2. BUBL is a:

(A)Portal   (B)Database
(C)OPAC   (D)Subject gateway

3. Who had given the "Minimal, Middling & Maximum" theories of reference service?

(A)Dr.S.R.Ranganathan   (B)S.Rothstein
(C)C.M.Winchell   (D)James I Wyer

4. "Compaction" is an important feature of:

(A)Indexes   (B)Bibliographies
(C)Reviews   (D)Market Report

5. The subject "Geophysics" has been formed as a result of:

(A)Agglomeration   (B)Fusion
(C)Fission   (D)Lamination

6. Arrange the following sources according to their date of origin:

(i)Social Science Index
(ii)Library Literature
(iii)Indian Library & Information Science Abstract
(iv)Library & Information Science Abstract

Codes:
(A)(iv)(i)(iii)(ii)   (B)(ii)(iv)(iii)(i)
(C)(iii)(i)(ii)(iv)   (D)(i)(iii)(ii)(iv)

7. Arrange the following reference sources according to their date of publication:

(i)Encyclopedia of Library & Information Science
(ii)McGraw Hill Encyclopedia of Science &Technology
(iii)Encyclopedia Americana
(iv)Encyclopedia Britannica

Codes:
(A)(i)(iv)(ii)(iii)   (B)(iv)(iii)(ii)(i)
(C)(ii)(iii)(iv)(i)   (D)(iii)(i)(ii)(iv)

8. Match the following:

| List-I | List-II |
| The Electronic Library | (i)USA |

List-I	List-II
(a)The Electronic Library	(i)USA
(b)Library Herald	(ii)Germany
(c)Library Trends	(iii)UK
(d)International Classification	(iv)India

Codes:
     (a)(b)(c)(d)
(A)(i)(iv)(iii)(ii)
(B)(ii)(i)(iv)(iii)
(C)(iv)(ii)(iii)(i)
(D)(iii)(iv)(i)(ii)

9. DARE, which is a UNESCO database, provides information for:

(A)Law   (B)Social Sciences
(C)Applied Sciences   (D)Pure Sciences

10. NALANDA, the digital library is an initiative of:

(A)NISCAIR   (B)DRTC
(C)NIT, Calicut   (D)IISC, Banglore

11. Identify the parts of "Social Science Citation Index":

(A)Corporate Index   (B)Permuterm Subject Index
(C)Source Index   (D)Title Index

Codes:
(i)A,B and C are correct   (ii)D,A and B are correct
(iii)B,C and D are correct   (iv)C,D and A are correct

12. "Delphi Technique" was first discussed in a monograph by:

(A)E.Nagel   (B)O.Helmer
(C)J.H.Shera   (D)D.M.Potter

13. "Noise" in information retrieval is due to:

(A)Recall value   (B)Precision
(C)Redundant Information   (D)Relevant Information

14. The concept of "Reference Service" was given by:

(A)Samuel Green   (B)A.Strauss
(C)J.H.Shera   (D)J.Martin

15. Database of "Research Synopses" is:

(A)Shodhganga   (B)Shodhgangotri
(C)Vidyanidhi   (D)NDL

16. INB is in how many parts?

(A)2   (B)3
(C)4   (D)1

17. The production of mental reflection and imagination is known as:

(A)Data   (B)Knowledge
(C)Information   (D)Idea

18. "Journal of Library & Information Science (JLIS)" is published from:

(A)Department of Library Science (DU)
(B)Department of Library Science (AMU)
(C)Department of Library Science (DRTC)
(D)Department of Library Science (IGNOU)

19. Access to the back volumes of electronic journals is known as:

(A)Random Access   (B)Perpetual Access
(C)Online Access   (D)Retrospective Access

20. Match the following:

        List-I   List-II
(a)Dictionary   (i)Foreign language
(b)Glossary   (ii)Synonymous terms
(c)Thesaurus   (iii)Words, Synonyms
(d)Lexicon   (iv)Specific subjects
Codes:
    (a)(b)(c)(d)
(A)(iv)(iii)(ii)(i)
(B)(iv)(ii)(i)(iii)
(C)(i)(ii)(iii)(iv)
(D)(iii)(iv)(ii)(i)

21. Match the following:

        List-I   List-II
(a)Fact on file   (i)Periodical directory
(b)World of
    learning   (ii)Index
(c)Concordance   (iii)Newpaper digest
(d)Willing's press
    guide   (iv)Directory

Codes:
    (a)(b)(c)(d)
(A)(iii)(iv)(ii)(i)
(B)(i)(ii)(iv)(iii)
(C)(i)(ii)(iii)(iv)

(D)(ii)(iii)(iv)(i)

22. Arrange the following indexing sources according to the year of
    their first publication:

(i)Biological Abstract   (ii)Chemical Abstract
(iii)Index Medicus   (iv)Pool's index to periodical literature

Codes:
(A)(iv)(ii)(i)(iii)   (B)(ii)(iii)(i)(iv)
(C)(i)(ii)(iv)(iii)   (D)(iv)(iii)(ii)(i)

23. Match the following:

        List-I   List-II
(a)Annals of Library   (i)S.R.E.L.S,
   & Info.Studies   Banglore
(b)Journal of Info.
   Management   (ii)DLA
(c)Herald of Library   (iii)NISCAIR
   Science
(d)Library Herald   (iv)Lucknow

Codes:
     (a)(b)(c)(d)
(A)(iii)(i)(iv)(ii)
(B)(i)(ii)(iii)(iv)
(C)(iv)(ii)(i)(iii)
(D)(ii)(i)(iv)(ii)

24. Match the following:

        List-I   List-II
(a)Barack Hussein   (i)Gazetteer
   Obama
(b)GDP growth in   (ii)Who's who
   last year
(c)Universities in   (iii)Year Book
   USA
(d)Area of Ganjam   (iv)World of learning
   district

Codes:
    (a)(b)(c)(d)
(A)(i)(ii)(iii)(iv)
(B)(iv)(ii)(i)(iii)
(C)(iii)(iv)(ii)(i)
(D)(ii)(iii)(iv)(i)

25. Match the following queries with appropriate category of Reference source:

List-I	List-II
(a) Enrolment of students in university	(i) Yearbook
(b) Weather of Denmark	(ii) Statistical source
(c) No.of foreigners visited world book fair in 2011	(iii) Directory
(d) No.of hospitals in India	(iv) Geographical source

Codes:
    (a)(b)(c)(d)
(A)(iii)(iv)(i)(ii)
(B)(iv)(iii)(i)(ii)
(C)(i)(iii)(ii)(iv)
(D)(ii)(iv)(i)(iii)

26. Match the following:

List-I	List-II
(a) User education	(i) James I Wyer
(b) Conservative, liberal & moderate theory of reference service	(ii) Patricia B Knapp
(c) Minimum, middling & maximum theory of reference	(iii) Eugene P Sheehy

service
(d)Guide to   (iv)S.Rothstein
reference book

Codes:
     (a)(b)(c)(d)
(A)(i)(ii)(iii)(iv)
(B)(ii)(iii)(iv)(i)
(C)(ii)(i)(iv)(iii)
(D)(iv)(iii)(i)(ii)

27. Match the following:

List-I	List-II
(a)Encyclopedia of associations	(i)Secondary sources
(b)Whitaker's almanac	(ii)Primary sources
(c)LISA	(iii)Directories
(d)The Economics Times	(iv)Yearbooks

Codes:
     (a)(b)(c)(d)
(A)(iii)(iv)(i)(ii)
(B)(i)(ii)(iii)(iv)
(C)(iv)(ii)(i)(iii)
(D)(ii)(i)(iii)(iv)

28. The initiation, selection, exploration, formulation, collection and
    presentation are two stages of which model of information
    seeking behaviour

(A)Ellis Model   (B)Krikelas Model
(C)Kuhlthou Model   (D)Wilson Model

29. Jubilee Project is associated with what?

(A)Evaluation of electronic information services
(B)Public library survey

(C)Strategic management of libraries
(D)Scale development

30. The publisher of "Information Power: Building Partnership for
    Learning" is:

(A)AASL   (B)AECT
(C)ALA   (D)ILA

31. 'CODEN' is connected with:

(A)Books   (B)Serials
(C)Reports   (D)Gray Literature

32. Roget's International Thesaurus is a:

(A)Classified List of Words   (B)Book of Synonyms
(C)List of Standard Terms   (D)List of Scientific Terms

33. Information about scale and projection can be found in

(A)Encyclopaedias   (B)Hand books of Manuals
(C)Geographical sources   (D)Directories

34. Who of the following is not the author of any reference book?

(A)C.M.Winchell   (B)William A.Katz
(C)Louis Shores   (D)Maurice B.Line

35. Which of the following is not a part of word treatment in language
    dictionaries?

(A)Gloss   (B)Vernacular
(C)Etymology   (D)Grammatical information

36. Which sources would you consult to know the "Impact Factor" of
    Journal publications?

(i)Web of Science   (ii)Science Direct
(iii)SCOPUS   (iv)EBSCO

Codes:
(A)(i) and (iv)   (B)(ii) and (iii)
(C)(i) and (iii)   (D)(iii) and (iv)

37. Science Citation Index is published by:

(A)Thomson Reuters   (B)H.W.Wilson
(C)Whitaker   (D)R.R.Bowker

38. Who was the Chairman of 'National Policy on Library &
    Information Systems' (1986)?

(A)D.N.Banerjee   (B)D.P.Chattopadhyay
(C)Sam Pitroda   (D)Kalpana Dasgupta

39. Digital Reference Service can be offered through:

(A)FAX   (B)OPAC
(C)Ask your librarian (D)Consortia

40. Which of the following are 'Inclusive geographical sources'?

(i)Maps   (ii)Atlases
(iii)Encyclopaedias   (iv)Yearbooks

Codes:
(A)(i) & (ii) are correct   (B)(iii) & (iv) are correct
(C)(ii) & (iii) are correct   (D)(ii) & (iv) are correct

41. Which of the following are not styles of citation?

(i)Anglo American Cataloguing Rules
(ii)MLA Handbook for Writers of Research Papers
(iii)Chicago Manual of Style
(iv)Little Science Big Science

Codes:
(A)(i) and (ii) are correct   (B)(iii) and (iv) are correct
(C)(i) and (iv) are correct   (D)(ii) and (iii) are correct

42. Arrange the following publications according to their year of origin:

(i)Social Science Citation Index
(ii)LISA
(iii)Library Literature and Information Science
(iv)Library Journal

Codes:
(A)(i)(iii)(iv)(ii)   (B)(ii)(i)(iii)(iv)
(C)(iv)(iii)(ii)(i)   (D)(iii)(ii)(iv)(i)

43. Arrange the following according to their year of first publication:

(i)Encyclopaedia Britannica
(ii)Encyclopaedia Americana
(iii)Encyclopaedia of Library and Information Science
(iv)McGraw-Hill Encyclopaedia of Science and Technology

Codes:
(A)(iv)(iii)(i)(ii)
(B)(i)(ii)(iv)(iii)
(C)(iii)(i)(iv)(ii)
(D)(ii)(iv)(i)(iii)

44. Who categorized the user studies into the following three
    categories?

(i)Behaviour Studies   (ii)Use studies.
(iii)Information flow studies

Options:
(A)Maurice B Line   (B)Menzel
(C)Cronin   (D)Voigt

45. The physical and chemical treatment of materials to retard their
    further deterioration refers to:

(A)Conservation   (B)Rescuing
(C)Prevention   (D)Restoration

46. NICRYS is information system for:

(A)Machine tools   (B)Food science
(C)Crystallography   (D)Drugs

47. Name of the President of Sri Lanka can be found in:

(A)International who's who   (B)Stateman's Yearbook
(C)Who's who in the world   (D)Wilson Biographies

48. Which of the following has stopped publishing in the print from
    since 2012?

(A)Europa World Yearbook
(B)Times of India Directory
(C)New Encyclopedia Britannica
(D)Keesing's Contemporary Archives

49. Which of the following is not providing encyclopaedia type of
    information?

(A)Encyclopedia of Associations
(B)Compton's Encyclopedia
(C)Worldbook Encyclopedia
(D)Encyclopedia Americana

50. Which of the following is not reference service?

(i)Preparation of user profile
(ii)Initiation of freshman
(iii)Compilation of document list
(iv)Readers Advisory

Codes:
(A)(i) and (ii)   (B)(ii) and (iii)
(C)(i) and (iii)   (D)(iii) and (iv)

51. Which of the following functions are analysed by ALA as reference
    service functions?

(i)Consultation function   (ii)Guidance function
(iii)Instruction function   (iv)Bibliographic function

Codes:
(A)(i)(ii) and (iii) are correct
(B)(ii)(iii) and (iv) are correct
(C)(i)(ii) and (iv) are correct
(D)(i)(iii) and (iv) are correct

52. Magazines are suitable for:

(i)Leisure and entertainment   (ii)Scholarly information
(iii)Popular information   (iv)Subject information

Codes:
(A)(i)(ii) and (iii) are correct
(B)(ii)(iii) and (iv) are correct
(C)(i) and (iii) are correct
(D)(ii) and (iv) are correct

53. Match the following:

List-I	List-II
(a)See	(i)ibid
(b)Previously cited	(ii)loc.cit
(c)Same reference cited immediately above	(iii)op.cit
(d)The same place cited	(iv)vide

Codes:
      (a)(b)(c)(d)
(A)(i)(ii)(iii)(iv)
(B)(ii)(i)(iv)(iii)
(C)(iii)(iv)(ii)(i)
(D)(iv)(iii)(i)(ii)

54. Match the following:

List-I	List-II
(a)Institutional repository	(i)Vidyanidhi
(b)Electronic theses & dissertations	(ii)TKDL
(c)Digital library of journals	(iii)DOAJ
(d)Digital archive	(iv)E-prints

Codes:
```
      (a)(b)(c)(d)
(A)(iv)(i)(iii)(ii)
(B)(i)(ii)(iii)(iv)
(C)(iii)(ii)(iv)(i)
(D)(ii)(iii)(i)(iv)
```

55. Match the following:

List-I	List-II
(a)User orientation service	(i)Bibliographic
(b)Information repackaging	(ii)Reference service
(c)Translation	(iii)Digest service
(d)Indexing	(iv)Support service

Codes:
```
      (a)(b)(c)(d)
(A)(i)(iv)(iii)(ii)
(B)(iii)(ii)(i)(iv)
(C)(iv)(i)(ii)(iii)
(D)(ii)(iii)(iv)(i)
```

56. 188. Walford's Guide to Reference Material is published by

(A)American Library Association, Chicago
(B)R.R. Bowker, London
(C)Library Association Publishing, London

(D)Learned Information Ltd., New Jersey

57.The word "Encyclopedia" is derived from which language?

(A)Greek   (B)Latin
(C)Persian   (D)English

58. The word "Dictionary" is derived from which language?

(A)Greek   (B)Latin
(C)Persian   (D)English

59. The word "Lexican" is derived from which language?

(A) English   (B)Latin
(C)Persian   (D)Greek

60.DELNET stands for:

(A)Developing Library Network
(B)Delhi Library Network
(C)Decrypting Library Network
(D)Demand for Library Network

61. "SDI" is an example of which type of reference service?

(A)On Demand   (B)Anticipative
(C)Referral   (D)ILL

62. "SDI" stands for:

(A)Selective Dissemination of Information
(B)Selective Demand of Information
(C)Selected Demand for Information
(D)Selection for Demand Information

63. "SDI" was invented in the year:

(A)1960   (B)1959
(C)1961   (D)1962

64. "SDI" was invented by:

(A)Ranganathan   (B)Melvil Dewey
(C)M.E.Cutter   (D)H.P.Luhn

65. "DDS" stands for:

(A)Document Delivery Service
(B)Document Demand Service
(C)Disseminative Demand Service
(D)Disseminative Delivery Service

66. "PIS" stands for:

(A)Public Information System
(B)Patent Information System
(C)Public Infomative System
(D)Parent Information System

67. "NISSAT" was developed in the year:

(A)1977   (B)1976
(C)1970   (D)1975

68. "NIC" was established in the year:

(A)1978   (B)1976
(C)1974   (D)1977

69. DELNET was started in the year:

(A)1988   (B)1989
(C)1992   (D)1994

70. "CEIS" stands for:

(A)Central Excise Information System
(B)Central Exercise Information System
(C)Control Excise Information System

Answers

1(B)	2(D)	3(B)	4(C)	5(B)	6(A)	7(B)	8(D)	9(B)
10(C)	11(i)	12(B)	13(C)	14(A)	15(B)	16(A)	17(D)	18(A)
19(B)	20(D)	21(A)	22(D)	23(A)	24(D)	25(A)	26(C)	27(A)
28(C)	29(A)	30(C)	31(B)	32(A)	33(C)	34(D)	35(A)	36(C)
37(A)	38(B)	39(C)	40(B)	41(C)	42(C)	43(B)	44(B)	45(A)
46(C)	47(B)	48(C)	49(A)	50(C)	51(C)	52(C)	53(C)	54(A)
55(D)	56(C)	57(A)	58(B)	59(D)	60(A)	61(A)	62(A)	63(C)
64(D)	65(A)	66(B)	67(A)	68(B)	69(A)	70(A)		

1. Arrange the following library automation software according to their date of origin:

(i)SOUL   (ii)KOHA
(iii)NewGenLib   (iv)LIBSYS

Codes:
(A)(i)(iv)(ii)(iii)   (B)(iii)(ii)(i)(iv)
(C)(i)(iii)(iv)(ii)   (D)(iv)(i)(ii)(iii)

2. The term "hyper text" was coined by:

(A)Ted Nelson   (B)Charles Babbage
(C)Tay Vaughan   (D)Tim Berner Lee

3. Conversion of barcode into electrical signals is done by:

(A)CRT   (B)Photo sensor
(C)UNICODE   (D)Scanners

4. The 12 rules for relational database were given by:

(A)J.Bill Gates   (B)e.f.Codd
(C)Larvy Page   (D)Linus Tolward

5. Match the following:

List-I	List-II
(a)Search Engine	(i)Pascal
(b)Browser	(ii)UNIX
(c)Operating System	(iii)Yahoo
(d)Programming Language	(iv)Netscape

Codes:
     (a)(b)(c)(d)
(A)(i)(ii)(iii)(iv)
(B)(ii)(i)(iv)(iii)

(C)(iv)(i)(ii)(iii)
(D)(iii)(iv)(ii)(i)

6. "Decoding" also refers to as:

(A)Encryption   (B)Password break
(C)Decryption   (D)Encoding

7. Which number denotes the Binary equivalent of "13"?

(A)1010   (B)1101
(C)1111   (D)1100

8. Computers can only understand the language of:

(A)C   (B)0 and 1
(C)1 and 0   (D)C++

9. Binary equivalent of 28 is:

(A)11100   (B)11000
(C)10100   (D)11101

10. Name the Scientist who said that "Information science is a cluster of many disciplines where the central core is 'Information':

(A)Fritz Machlup   (B)B.C.Brooks
(C)N.J.Belkin   (D)Daniel Bell

11. Who coined the term "Information Retrieval"?

(A)Calvin Moores   (B)Dr.S.R.Ranganathan
(C)H.P.Luhn   (D)J.D.Brown

12. Who is the propounder of the tem "Information Transfer"?

(A)Bissman   (B)J.Martin
(C)J.H.Shera   (D)C.Moores

13. Web impact factor was developed by:

(A)R.Rousseau   (B)M.Thelwall
(C)L.Bornebora   (D)P.Ingwersen

14. Match the following:

     List-I   List-II
(a)My SQL   (i)Language
(b)Apache   (ii)Server
(c)Ada   (iii)User interface
(d)API   (iv)RDBMS

Codes:
      (a)(b)(c)(d)
(A)(iv)(ii)(i)(iii)
(B)(i)(ii)(iv)(iii)
(C)(ii)(i)(iii)(iv)
(D)(iii)(ii)(i)(iv)

15. In Binary number system digit "21" is represented by:

(A)11010   (B)10101
(C)11001   (D)10011

16. template is a:

(A)Recursive routine   (B)I/O measurement
(C)Assembler program   (D)Structured specification

17. "DOI" stand for:

(A)Duplex Object Identifier
(B)Digital Object Identification
(C)Digital Object Identifier
(D)Double Object Identification

18. "UNIVAC" is an example of which generation of computers?
(A)2nd generation   (B)1st generation
(C)3rd generation   (D)5th generation

19. "Vacuum Tubes" were used in which generation of computers?

(A)1st generation   (B)4th generation
(C)5th generation   (D)2nd generation

20. "Transistors" were used in which generation of computers?

(A)2nd generation   (B)1st generation
(C)3rd generation   (D)5th generation

21. "UNIVAC-1108" is an example of which generation of computers?

(A)5th generation   (B)1st generation
(C)3rd generation   (D)2nd generation

22. "Integrated Circuits (ICs)" were used in which generation of computers?

(A)5th generation   (B)1st generation
(C)3rd generation   (D)2nd generation

23. "Honeywell" is an example of which generation of computers?

(A)5th generation   (B)1st generation
(C)2nd generation   (D)3rd generation

24. "Very Large Scale Integrated Circuits Chips (VLSICC)" is used in which generation of computers?

(A)1st generation   (B)4th generation
(C)5th generation   (D)2nd generation

25. "Desktop" is an example of which generation of computers?
(A)2nd generation   (B)1st generation
(C)3rd generation   (D)4th generation

26. "Artificial Intelligence (AI)" is used in which generation of computers?
(A)5th generation   (B)1st generation
(C)2nd generation   (D)3rd generation

27. "Robotics" is an example of which generation of computers?

(A)1st generation   (B)4th generation
(C)5th generation   (D)2nd generation

28. "ENIAC, EDVAC, IBM-650 & IBM-701" are an example of which
    generation of computers?

(A)1st generation   (B)4th generation
(C)5th generation   (D)2nd generation

29. "CDC-1604, CDC-3600, IBM-1620 & IBM-7094" are an example of
    which generation of computers?

(A)1st generation   (B)4th generation
(C)5th generation   (D)2nd generation

30. "TDC-316, IBM-360 & IBM-370" are an example of which
    generation of computers?

(A)1st generation   (B)3rd generation
(C)5th generation   (D)2nd generation

31. "Laptop, Notebook & Ultrabook" are an example of which
    generation of computers?

(A)1st generation   (B)4th generation
(C)5th generation   (D)2nd generation

32. "Weather forecasting, Neural network & Satellite communication"
    are an example of which generation of computers?

(A)1st generation   (B)3rd generation
(C)5th generation   (D)2nd generation

33. An "operating system" is also known as:

(A)Application software   (B)System software
(C)Windows   (D)Macintosh

34. Which among the following is a "Command Based" operating system?

(A)LINUX   (B)UNIX
(C)DOS   (D) All of the above

35. Which among the following is a "Graphics Based" operating system?

(A)Windows   (B)Macintosh
(C)UBANTU   (D)All of the above

36. "Real-Time, Time-Sharing, Networked & Distributed" are the types of:

(A)System software   (B)Application software
(C)Windows   (D)Macintosh

37. Which among the following is a function of an "operating system"?

(A)Resource Management   (B)Memory Management
(C)Process Management   (D)All of the above

38. "I/O Management, File Management, Program Execution & Error Handling" are the functions of:

(A)Operating system   (B)Application software
(C)Linux   (D)Windows

39. Arrange these versions of windows in their chronological order:

(i)Window 7   (ii)Window Vista
(iii)Window XP   (iv)Window 8

Codes:
(A)(i) (ii) (ii) (iv)   (B)(iii) (ii) (i) (iv)
(C)(ii) (iii) (iv) (i)   (D)(iv) (i) (ii) (iii)

40. "Cloud Computing" is basically a concept of:

(A)Spotlight   (B)Virtual Database
(C)Boot up   (D)Sleep mode

41. Which among the following is "Library Automation Software"?

(A)PMB   (B)Horizon
(C)Unicorn   (D)All of the above

42. "ILMS" stands for:

(A)Indian Library Management System
(B)Integrated Library Management Software
(C)India Library Management Software
(D)Integrated Library Management System

43. Which among the following is a "Foreign Origin" ILMS?

(A)Virtua   (B)LibSys
(C)SOUL   (D)NEXLIB

44. Which among the following are some examples of ILMS?

(A)e-Granthalya   (B)AutoLIB
(C)SLIMZI   (D)All of the above

45. Which among the following is an "Open Source" Library
    Automation Software?

(A)Koha   (B)SOUL
(C)NewGenLib   (D)All of the above

46. Which among the following is a "Foreign Origin" ILMS?

(A)ALICE   (B)NG-TLMS.net
(C)LAMP   (D)All of the above

47. "Cray-Jaguar, Cray-I, Cray-II & IBM-roadrunner" are some
    examples of:

(A)Mainframes   (B)Supercomputers
(C)Minicomputers   (D)Microcomputers

48. "IBM-Z9, IBM-Z10 & Enterprise Servers" are some examples of:

(A)Mainframes   (B)Supercomputers
(C)Minicomputers   (D)Microcomputers

49. "IBM, Lenovo, HP & Dell" are some examples of:

(A)Mainframes   (B)Supercomputers
(C)Minicomputers   (D)Microcomputers

50. "Laptop, Desktop, PDA & Palmtop" are some examples of:

(A)Mainframes   (B)Supercomputers
(C)Minicomputers   (D)Microcomputers

51. An invisible college is a typical example of:

(A)Informal channels of communication
(B)Formal channels of communication
(C)Both (A) and (B)
(D)None of the above

52. FID was dissolved in the year:

(A)2005   (B)2000
(C)2002   (D)2003

53. Arrange the following online systems in the order of their origin:

(i)ERIC   (ii)MEDLINE
(iii)OCLC   (iv)MARC

Codes:
(A)(i)(iii)(ii)(iv)   (B)(i)(iv)(iii)(ii)
(C)(ii)(i)(iii)(iv)   (D)(ii)(iii)(i)(iv)

54. Berne convention was adopted in the year:

(A)1912   (B)1986
(C)1950   (D)1900

55. S.M.C.R. communication model was developed by:

(A)Charles Osgood   (B)W.Schramm
(C)David K.Berlo   (D)Harold Lasswell

56. Information For All Programme (IFAP) was launched by:

(A)UNESCO   (B)OCLC
(C)IFLA   (D)Library of Congress

57. Whose model of communication of knowledge suggests that
    communication is an open system?

(A)M. Foucault   (B)Shannon & weaver
(C)J.Hebermans   (D)G.Garbner

58. The concept of "Knowledge Industry" was introduced by:

(A)Fritz Machlup   (B)P.Drucker
(C)W.Saffady   (D)Marc Porat

59. The place where IFLA was found:

(A)London   (B)Hague, Netherlands
(C)Finland   (D)Edinburg, Scotland

60. "ILP" stands for:

(A)International Literacy Programme
(B)Indian Language Preogramme
(C)Information Literacy Programme
(D)Infomation Language Programme

61. "UAP" stands for:

(A)Uniform Access to Publications
(B)Universal Availability of Publications
(C)Unicode Access to Publications
(D)Union Apograph Publications

62. "FRBR" was developed by:

(A)IFLA   (B)UNESCO
(C)LC   (D)FID

63. In 1974, Zurkowski used for the first time which of the following
    term?

(A)Digital Literacy   (B)Media Literacy
(C)Computer Literacy   (D)Information Literacy

64. Inference Engine is a part of which information system?

(A)Management information System
(B)Decision Support System
(C)Expert System
(D)Open System

65. The information network that connects Universities and Colleges in
    United Kingdom :

(A)JANET   (B)SERCNET
(C)OCLC   (D)BONET

66. Internet filtering is

(A)A form of censorship
(B)Acceptable user policy
(C)Access to inappropriate material
(D)Blocking internet facility

67. Which one of the following is a Bulletin Board Service on Internet?

(A)Picaso   (B)Google talk
(C)Blog   (D)Oovoo

68. Virus is software which can:

(A)Manipulate data   (B)Replicate itself
(C)Damage computer   (D)All the above

69. Which one of the following protocol is used in file transfer over internet?

(A)FTP   (B)SMTP
(C)POP   (D)TCP/IP

70. Blair and Maron evaluation study on retrieval effectiveness of full
     text search is called:

(A)SMART Retrieval Experiment
(B)MEDLARS evaluation study
(C)STAIRS project
(D)Cranefield-II Project

71. Even though 'Xerography' is a photocopying method, but it is
     called:

(A)Diazographic   (B)Thermographic
(C)Electrofax   (D)Electrostatic

72. Identify the odd one out.

(A)ANSI   (B)BIS
(C)BSI   (D)ESPN

73. Which of the following is not the prerequisite for a National
     Information Policy?

(A)Legislative Frame work
(B)Production of National Bibliography

(C)Advisory and Administrative body
(D)ICT infrastructure facilities

74. World Intellectual Property Organization is related to:

(A)UNESCO   (B)United Nations
(C)U.S.Organization   (D)International Law Organization

75. Redundancy of information is:

(A)Unnecessary and should be eliminated
(B)Unnecessary but cannot be avoided
(C)Necessary and sometimes useful
(D)Necessary and always desirable

76. Radio Frequency Identification is used in library for:

(i)Circulation of Documents
(ii)Cataloguing of Documents
(iii)Security of Documents
(iv)Acquisition of Documents

Codes:
(A)(i) and (ii) are correct   (B)(ii) and (iv) are correct
(C)(iii) and (ii) are correct   (D)(i) and (iii) are correct

77. BIOS contain:

(i)Operating System Program
(ii)Bootstrap Program
(iii)Application System Program
(iv)Convert Character to Code Program

Codes:
(A)(i) and (ii) are correct   (B)(ii) and (iii) are correct
(C)(iii) and (iv) are correct   (D)(ii) and (iv) are correct

78. In the information transfer cycles, internet is acting as:

(i)Primary Publisher   (ii)Secondary Publisher (iii)Tertiary Publisher   (iv)Primary Distributor

Codes:
(A)(i)(iii)and(iv)are correct.   (B)(i)(ii)and(iv)are correct
(C)(ii)(iii)and(iv)are correct   (D)(i)(ii)and(iii)are correct

79. Match the following:

List-I	List-II
(a)HTML File	(i)Text Format
(b)PDF File	(ii)Film Format
(c)JPG File	(iii)Web Format
(d)AVI File	(iv)Image Format

Codes:
        (a)(b)(c)(d)
(A)(i)(ii)(iv)(iii)
(B)(iii)(i)(iv)(ii)
(C)(i)(iv)(ii)(iii)
(D)(iv)(iii)(i)(ii)

80. Match the following:

List-I	List-II
(a)ILMS	(i)Drupal
(b)Digital library software	(ii)Moodle
(c)Content management software	(iii)Dspace
(d)Learning management software	(iv)NewGenLib

Codes:
        (a)(b)(c)(d)
(A)(iv)(iii)(ii)(i)
(B)(ii)(i)(iv)(iii)
(C)(iii)(iv)(ii)(i)
(D)(i)(ii)(iii)(iv)

81. Match the following:

List-I	List-II
(a)Video networking site	(i)Facebook
(b)Social networking site	(ii)Researchgate
(c)Academic networking site	(iii)Oovoo
(d)Photo networking site	(iv)Flicker

Codes:

   (a)(b)(c)(d)
(A)(i)(iii)(ii)(iv)
(B)(iv)(i)(ii)(iii)
(C)(ii)(iii)(i)(iv)
(D)(iii)(iv)(i)(ii)

82. Relational Database is:

(A)A work which has some relationship to another work
(B)A symbol representing relationship between two concepts
(C)Manipulation commands which relate records in different fields
(D)All of the above

83. "Internet Public Library" is being maintained by

(A)MIT, Massachusettes   (B)University of Michigan
(C)University of Arizona   (D)Drexal University

84. What are the major driving forces behind an 'Information society'?

(i)R.T.I   (ii)I.C.T.
(iii)Internet   (iv)I.T.ACT

Codes:
(A)(ii)&(i) are correct   (B)(ii)&(iv) are correct
(C)(i)&(iv) are correct   (D)(ii)&(iii) are correct

85. The factors that influence computer file organisation are:

(i) Speed of access   (ii) Storage space
(iii) Fixed length fields   (iv) File volatility

Codes:
(A) (i)(ii) and (iii) are correct   (B) (i)(ii) and (iv) are correct
(C) (ii)(iii) and (iv) are correct   (D) (i)(iii) and (iv) are correct

86. Major problems of 'Information Communication Technology' are

(i) Information overload
(ii) Information insecurity
(iii) Lack of innovative technologies
(iv) Lack of control over communication

Codes:
(A) (ii) and (iv) are correct   (B) (i) and (iv) are correct
(C) (i)(ii) and (iv) are correct   (D) (i)(ii) and (iii) are correct

87. Which of the following are 'Open Source Content Management Systems'?

(i) Drupal   (ii) Atex
(iii) Joomla   (iv) OpenCms

Codes:
(A) (i)(ii) and (iv) are correct   (B) (i)(ii) and (iii) are correct
(C) (ii)(iii) and (iv) are correct   (D) (i)(iii) and (iv) are correct

88. Arrange the following according to their year of enactment in India:

(i) Freedom of Information Act
(ii) Right to Information Act
(iii) Copyright Act (Revised)
(iv) Information Technology Act

Codes:
(A) (iv)(ii)(i)(iii)   (B) (iii)(iv)(i)(ii)

(C)(ii)(iii)(iv)(i)   (D)(i)(iv)(ii)(iii)

89. Match the following:

List-I	List-II
(a)Textual representation	(i)Pascal
(b)Computer language	(ii)Gopher
(c)Network tool	(iii)Boolean
(d)Search technique	operator
	(iv)ASCII

Codes:
     (a)(b)(c)(d)
(A)(iv)(i)(ii)(iii)
(B)(i)(iv)(iii)(ii)
(C)(iii)(ii)(iv)(i)
(D)(ii)(iv)(iii)(i)

90. Who defined "to be information literate, a person must be able to
    recognize when information is needed and have the ability to
    locate, evaluate and use effectively the needed information."?

(A)SLA   (B)ALA
(C)IFLA   (D)CILIP

91. National Knowledge Network is to be implemented by:

(A)National Knowledge Commission
(B)Information and Library Network
(C)National Information Centre
(D)Department of Information Technology

92. Metadata Dublin core refers to:

(A)Data elements in database
(B)Bibliographic elements in database
(C)Field elements in database
(D)Subject elements in database

93. E-Journal artides can be identified with the help of:

(A)Digital Journal Identifier
(B)Journal Source Identifier
(C)Journal Article Identifier
(D)Digital Object Identifier

94. Z39.50 is a standard for:

(A)Communication formats
(B)Search and Retrieval services
(C)Cataloguing Web Resources
(D)Library Management Services

95. In context to modulation, PCM stands for:

(A)Pulse Code Modulation
(B)Phase Control Modulation
(C)Popular Code Modulation
(D)Penultimate Code Modulation

96. Digital library function incorporate:

(i)Creating and capturing
(ii)Storage and management
(iii)Search and access
(iv)Abstracting and reviewing

Codes:
(A)(i)(ii)and(iii) are correct   (B)(i)(iii)and(iv) are correct
(C)(ii)(iii)and(iv) are correct   (D)(i)(ii)and(iv) are correct

97. Which topology of computer network provides faster server
    access?

(i)BUS network topology
(ii)RING network topology
(iii)MULTIPLE RING network topology
(iv)STAR network topology

Codes:
(A)(i)and(ii) are correct   (B)(i)and(iii) are correct
(C)(ii)and(iii) are correct   (D)(ii)and(iv) are correct

98. Which of the following are ISDN services?

(i)RSS   (ii)Teletext
(iii)Voice mail   (iv)Video conference

Codes:
(A)(i)(iii)and(iv) are correct   (B)(i)(ii)and (iv) are correct
(C)(ii)(iii)and(iv) are correct   (D)(i)(ii)and(iii) are correct

99. Which of the following are the problems of present information
    environment?

(i)Information indiscipline   (ii)Information literacy
(iii)Information overload   (iv)Information technology

Codes:
(A)(i)and(iii) are correct   (B)(i)and(iv) are correct
(C)(ii)and(iv) are correct   (D)(i)and(ii) are correct

100. Match the following:

        List-I   List-II
(a)Informix   (i)Image software
(b)Omnipage   (ii)Remote login
(c)Tiff viewer   software
(d)Team viewer   (iii)DBMS software
                               (iv)OCR software
Codes:
     (a)(b)(c)(d)
(A)(ii)(i)(iii)(iv)
(B)(iii)(iv)(i)(ii)
(C)(i)(ii)(iii)(iv)
(D)(iv)(iii)(ii)(i)

101. Match the following:

	List-I		List-II
(a)	Subject search engine	(i)	Altavista
(b)	Meta search engine	(ii)	Lycos
(c)	Regional search engine	(iii)	Geoindex
(d)	General search engine	(iv)	Savvysearch

Codes:

```
     (a)(b)(c)(d)
(A)(iii)(ii)(i)(iv)
(B)(iii)(iv)(ii)(i)
(C)(iii)(iv)(ii)(i)
(D)(iv)(ii)(iii)(i)
```

102. Which set of rules is applicable for exchange of files over Internet?

(A)FTP	(B)HTTP
(C)HTML	(D)IP

103. Which of the following is not a language of DBMS?

(A)DDL	(B)DML
(C)PASCAL	(D)PIL

104. "Information Literacy Competency Standards for Higher Education" is prepared by:

(A)AASL	(B)IFLA
(C)SCONUL	(D)ACRL

105. Name the storage medium compatible with speed of CPU for storing instructions or data temporarily during processing is:

(A)RAM	(B)ROM
(C)Cache	(D)EPROM

106. LAMP stands for:

(A) Library Archives Management Programme
(B) Laser Analysis and Multimedia Performance
(C) Linux Apache MySQL Perl
(D) Library Automation Management Protocol

107. Which of the following is not a database object?

(A) Tables   (B) Queries
(C) Relationships   (D) Reports

108. What is the process of transferring software programme from secondary storage media to the hard disc called?

(A) Download   (B) Upload
(C) Installation   (D) Storage

109. Name a technique used for searching stored data in a database:

(A) Boolean operator   (B) Inverting file
(C) Indexing   (D) Binary

110. The term 'Cyberspace' was first used by:

(A) G.Garbner   (B) William Gibson
(C) P.Tylor   (D) Ted Nelson

111. When CD-ROM was made:

(A) 1980   (B) 1982
(C) 1984   (D) 1985

112. Which of the following is not a social book marking site?

(A) Sqidoo   (B) Digg
(C) Facebook   (D) Delicious

113. PLONE is a:

(A)ILMS   (B)Content management system
(C)Operating system   (D)Digital library software

114. "Pi" is an e-book reading device by:

(A)LibSys   (B)Microsoft
(C)Infibeam   (D)Infonet

115.Which is a library management software for small libraries?

(A)Follet   (B)LibSys
(C)Alice   (D)PMB

116. Which is an example of "Micro blogging":

(A)Facebook   (B)Sqidoo
(C)Google   (D)Twitter

117. Microsoft Access is a:

(A)RDBMS   (B)OODBMS
(C)ORDBMS   (D)Network Database Model

118. A column in a Microsoft Access table is called?

(A)Row   (B)Record
(C)Field   (D)Column

119. Which key Uniquely Identifies each record in Database?

(A)Primary key   (B)Key record
(C)Unique key   (D)Field name

120. In a Database Table, category of information is called:

(A)Tuple   (B)Field
(C)Record   (D)All of the above

Answers

1(D)	2(A)	3(D)	4(B)	5(D)	6(C)	7(B)	8(B)	9(A)
10(A)	11(A)	12(A)	13(D)	14(A)	15(B)	16(D)	17(C)	18(B)
19(A)	20(A)	21(D)	22(C)	23(D)	24(B)	25(D)	26(A)	27(C)
28(A)	29(D)	30(B)	31(B)	32(C)	33(B)	34(D)	35(D)	36(A)
37(D)	38(A)	39(B)	40(B)	41(D)	42(B)	43(A)	44(D)	45(D)
46(D)	47(B)	48(A)	49(C)	50(D)	51(A)	52(C)	53(B)	54(B)
55(C)	56(A)	57(D)	58(A)	59(D)	60(C)	61(B)	62(A)	63(D)
64(C)	65(A)	66(A)	67(C)	68(D)	69(A)	70(C)	71(D)	72(D)
73(B)	74(B)	75(A)	76(D)	77(D)	78(B)	79(B)	80(C)	81(C)
82(C)	83(D)	84(D)	85(B)	86(C)	87(D)	88(B)	89(A)	90(B)
91(C)	92(A)	93(D)	94(B)	95(A)	96(A)	97(D)	98(C)	99(C)
100(B)	101(C)	102(B)	103(C)	104(D)	105(C)	106(C)	107(C)	
108(C)	109(A)	110(B)	111(D)	112(A)	113(B)	114(C)	115(A)	
116(D)	117(A)	118(B)	119(A)	120(B)				

Administration & Management in Library & Information Science

1. ZBB was developed by:

(A)C.V.Good   (B)Peter A.Pyhrr
(C)Dr.S.R.Ranganathan   (D)R.D.Stuart

2. "PERT" was developed by:

(A)Booz-Allen Hamelton
(B)The Navy special project office
(C)Both (A) and (B)
(D)None of the above

3. "Milian Book Project" was initiated by:

(A)MIT, USA
(B)Carnegie Mellon University
(C)Pittsburg University
(D)Michigan University

4. "Granthana" is an official publication of:

(A)RRRLF   (B)ILA
(C)IASLIC   (D)APLA

5. Match the following:

List-I	List-II
(a) Principles of Management	(i)F.W.Taylor
(b) Functions of Management	(ii)Abraham Maslow
(c) Theory of Hierarchy of needs	(iii)Luther Gullick
(d) Schools of Management	(iv)Henry Fayol

Codes:
    (a)(b)(c)(d)
(A)(ii)(i)(iv)(iii)
(B)(iv)(iii)(ii)(i)
(C)(i)(iii)(ii)(iv)
(D)(i)(ii)(iv)(iii)

6. Match the following:

List-I	List-II
(a) McGroger Theory X	(i) Less external control
(b) McGroger Theory Y	(ii) PERT
(c) Unity of command	(iii) Worker's participation in decision making
(d) Time and cost	(iv) All powers in one person

Codes:
    (a)(b)(c)(d)
(A)(i)(ii)(iii)(iv)
(B)(iii)(i)(iv)(ii)
(C)(iv)(ii)(iii)(i)
(D)(ii)(i)(iii)(iv)

7. Match the following:

List-I	List-II
(a) W.Edward Deming	(i) Quality control circle
(b) Joseph M. Juran	(ii) TQM
(c) Armand V. Feigenbaum	(iii) Planning, Control, Improvement
(d) K.Ishikava	(iv) PDCA

Codes:
    (a)(b)(c)(d)
(A)(i)(ii)(iii)(iv)

(B)(iv)(iii)(ii)(i)
(C)(ii)(i)(iii)(iv)
(D)(iii)(ii)(iv)(i)

8. Which commission suggested that "6.5% to 10% of the total
   education budget of the country should spend for the development
   of 'University Libraries'?

(A)UGC commission   (B)Kothari commission
(C)Ranganathan commission (D)Sengupta commission

9. Which commission suggested that "6% of the total school
   expenditure should spend for the development of 'School Library'?

(A)Kothari commission   (B)UGC commission
(C)Ranganathan commission   (D)Sengupta commission

10. Which 'Budget estimation method' suggests "Rs.25 per student &
    Rs.300 per teacher" for making annual budget of a 'University
    Library'?

(A)Descriptive method   (B)Lump sum method
(C)Proportional method   (D)Per capita method

11. Which 'Budget estimation method' suggests "Rs.50 per student &
    Rs.150 per teacher" for making annual budget of a 'School
    Library'?

(A)Per capita method   (B)Lump sum method
(C)Proportional method   (D)Descriptive method

12. Which 'Budget estimation method' suggests "Rs.15 per student &
    Rs.200 per teacher" for making annual budget of a 'University
    Library'?

(A)Per capita method   (B)Lump sum method
(C)Proportional method   (D)Descriptive method

13. "Proportional Method & Per Capita Method of Budget Estimation"
    was given by:

(A)University Grants commission
(B)Ranganathan commission
(C)Kothari commission
(D)Sengupta commission

14. "Descriptive Method of Budget Estimation" was given by:

(A)University Grants commission
(B)Ranganathan commission
(C)Kothari commission
(D)Sengupta commission

15. Scaler chain shows:

(A) Authority structure
(B) Scale of performance of staff
(C) Chain for locating racks
(D) A link in the chain

16. 'Segmentation' is associated with

(A)Reference Service   (B)Market Survey Report
(C)Digest Service   (D)Indexing Service

17. State of the art report generally highlights

(A)General Aspects   (B)Technical Aspects
(C)Administrative Aspects   (D)All of the above

18. Methods and Techniques of Human Resource Planning includes:

(i)Selection and Recruitment
(ii)Induction and Placement
(iii)Quality Management
(iv)Performance Evaluation

Codes:
(A)(i)(iv) & (iii) are correct
(B)(iv)(iii) & (i) are correct
(C)(i)(ii) & (iv) are correct
(D)(iii) and (i) are correct

19. Which of the following are Schools of Management thought?

(i)Scientific Management School
(ii)Human Behavioural School
(iii)Classical School
(iv)School of Authority

Codes:
(A)(ii) and (iv) are correct
(B)(i)(ii) and (iv) are correct
(C)(iii) and (iv) are correct
(D)(i)(ii) and (iii) are correct

20. ISO 9000 standard denotes the

(A)Consistence confirmance of a product or service to a given set of
    standard or expectations
(B)Total customer satisfaction
(C)Representation of stakeholders issues.
(D)Detailed list of measuring techniques

21. The stages in the product life cycle curve are

(A)Introduction, Growth, Maturity, Decline
(B)Introduction, Growth, Maturity, Profit
(C)Growth, Maturity, Profit, Decline
(D)Introduction, Growth, Maturity, Saturation

22. Report on 'the development of digital libraries of the past decade'
    is categorized as:

(A)Review Report   (B)Trend Report
(C)Research Report   (D)State of the art report

23. Match the following:

List-I	List-II
(a)Right man at right library	(i)Annual financial statement
(b)Budget	(ii)Deployment
(c)Journal	(iii)TQM

(d)Identifying   (iv)ISSN
user's view
& expectations

Codes:
    (a)(b)(c)(d)
(A)(iii)(i)(ii)(iv)
(B)(ii)(i)(iv)(iii)
(C)(iv)(ii)(iii)(i)
(D)(i)(iii)(iv)(ii)

24. Match the following:

List-I   List-II
(a)Classical   (i)John Cotton
school   Danna
(b)X & Y   (ii)Henry
theory   Fayol
(c)Newark   (iii)Peter
charging   Drucker
system
(d)MBO   (iv)Douglas
                         McGregor
Code:
    (a)(b)(c)(d)
(A)(i)(iii)(iv)(ii)
(B)(iii)(iv)(i)(ii)
(C)(ii)(iv)(i)(iii)
(D)(iii)(ii)(iv)(i)

25. Match the following:

List-I   List-II
(a)Transaction   (i)Lower level
processing   managers
(b)Operational   (ii)Clerical
control   staff
(c)Management   (iii)Top level
control managers
(d)Strategic   (iv)Middle level
planning   managers

Codes:

     (a)(b)(c)(d)
(A)(iii)(ii)(iv)(i)
(B)(ii)(i)(iv)(iii)
(C)(iv)(ii)(iii)(i)
(D)(i)(ii)(iv)(iii)

26. Who coined the term POSDCORB?

(A)Luther Gullick   (B)F.W.Taylor
(C)Henri Fayol   (D)Max Weber

27. Who is considered is the father of "Scientific Management"?

(A)Luther Gullick   (B)F.W.Taylor
(C)Henri Fayol   (D)Max Weber

28. Management By Objectives (MBO) was given by:

(A)Peter Drucker   (B)F.W.Taylor
(C)Henri Fayol   (D)Max Weber

29. Manegement Process Theory (MPT) was given by:

(A)Beccan   (B)Charles
(C)Henry Fayol   (D)Hawthorne

30. "Formalistic Approach of Management" was given by:

(A)Peter Drucker   (B)F.W.Taylor
(C)Henri Fayol   (D)Max Weber

31. "Theory of Motivation" was given by:

(A)Marslaw
(B)Herzberg
(C)Henry Fayol
(D)Hawthorne

32. "Theory of Hierarchy of Needs" was given by:

(A) Marslaw
(B) Herzberg
(C) Henry Fayol
(D) Hawthorne

33. "MBO" was given by Peter Drucker in the year:

(A) 1950   (B) 1951
(C) 1953   (D) 1954

34. Drury's principle of book selection was given in the year:

(A) 1930   (B) 1932
(C) 1933   (D) 1934

35. The principle of book selection "To provide right book to right
    reader at right time" was given by:

(A) Melvil Dewey
(B) Drury
(C) Ranganathan
(D) McColvin

36. The principle of book selection "Best reading to largest number at
    least cost" was given by:

(A) Melvil Dewey
(B) Drury
(C) Ranganathan
(D) McColvin

37. The principle of book selection on the basis of "Demand & Supply"
    was given by:

(A) Melvil Dewey
(B) Drury
(C) Ranganathan
(D) McColvin

38. Which among the following is the best principle of book selection
    for libraries, according to the LIS experts?

(A) Dewey's principle
(B) Drury's principle
(C) Ranganathan's principle
(D) McColvin's principle

39. The ultimate responsibility of book selection rests with the:

(A) Librarian
(B) Advisory committee
(C) Vice chancellor
(D) Acquisition staff

40. An estimate of revenue & expenditure for the coming financial
    year is called:

(A) Zero budget
(B) Statistics
(C) Budget
(D) Report

Answers

1(B)	2(B)	3(B)	4(A)	5(B)	6(B)	7(B)	8(B)	9(A)
10(D)	11(A)	12(D)	13(C)	14(A)	15(A)	16(B)	17(B)	18(C)
19(D)	20(A)	21(A)	22(B)	23(B)	24(C)	25(B)	26(A)	27(B)
28(A)	29(C)	30(D)	31(B)	32(A)	33(D)	34(A)	35(B)	36(A)
37(D)	38(B)	39(A)	40(C)					

1. "Ranganathan's spiral of Scientific Research" has how many 'Quadrants'?

(A)4   (B)3
(C)5   (D)6

2. Match the following:

List-I	List-II
(a)Law of scattering	(i)Zipf' Law
(b)Measurement of word frequency	(ii)Eugene Garfield
(c)Measurement of Author's productivity	(iii)Bradford's Law
(d)Impact factor	(iv)Latka's Law

Codes:
    (a)(b)(c)(d)
(A)(ii)(iv)(i)(iii)
(B)(iv)(iii)(ii)(i)
(C)(i)(ii)(iii)(iv)
(D)(iii)(i)(iv)(ii)

3. Gotam's book "Nyasutra" has given the following four steps of scientific research.Arrange them in proper order:

(i)Verification/Testing (Aptavakshya)
(ii)Comparison (Upaman)
(iii)Inference (Anuman)
(iv)Perception (Pratyaksha)

Codes:
(A)(ii)(iv)(i)(iii)   (B)(i)(iv)(ii)(iii)
(C)(iv)(ii)(iii)(i)   (D)(iv)(iii)(ii)(i)

4. External and Internal criticism implies in:

(A)Applied Research   (B)Experimental Research
(C)Survey Research   (D)Historical Research

5. Which of the following is not related to case study approach in a
   research design?

(A)Indepth Study
(B)Study of one/limited cases
(C)General study
(D)Little concern about generalisation to a large population

6. "Students' visit to Library is influenced by the availability of
   Internet". State "Students' visit to library" is which kind of
   variable?

(A)Independent Variable   (B)Intervening Variable
(C)Dependent Variable   (D)Intercept Variable

7. Research is conducted to:

(i)Generate new knowledge
(ii)Develop a theory
(iii)Develop communication skills
(iv)Re-interpret existing knowledge

Codes:

(A)(i)(iii) and (ii) are correct
(B)(iii)(ii) and (i) are correct
(C)(i)(ii) and (iv) are correct
(D)(i)(iii) and (iv) are correct

8. Which of the following tests can be employed for hypothesis
   testing?

(A)f-test   (B)Chi-square test
(C)t-test   (D)All of the above

9. Arrange the following according to their year of origin:

(i)Bradford's Law   (ii)Lotka's Law
(iii)Statistical Bibliography   (iv)Zipf's Law

Codes:
(A)(i)(iii)(iv)(ii)   (B)(i)(ii)(iv)(iii)
(C)(iv)(iii)(i)(ii)   (D)(iii)(ii)(iv)(i)

10. Idiographic hypothesis is directed towards predicting the
behaviour of:

(A)An Individual   (B)Group of People
(C)Masses   (D)People from same school of thought

11. In the process of reasoning when we start with a specific
statement, and conclude to a general statement, it is called:

(A)Deductive Reasoning   (B)Inductive Reasoning
(C)Abnormal Reasoning   (D)Transcendental Reasoning

12. Solomon Four group design is related to:

(A)Field studies
(B)Pretest post test control group design
(C)Data Analysis Model
(D)Statistical Technique

13. Which of the factor is not helping in limiting the external validity?

(A)Reactive effect
(B)Ecological validity
(C)Interaction between selection biases of experimental variables
(D)Ecological effect

14. Semantic differential scale is concerned with:

(A)Pool of items   (B)Selection from two opposite positions
(C)Five point scale   (D)Selection from a check list

15. In spiral of scientific method, the span of Zenith to Descendent is:

(A)Empirical phase   (B)Hypothesizing phase
(C)Deductive phase   (D)Verification phase

16. Which of the following variable cannot be expressed in
    quantitative terms?

(A)Socio-Economic status   (B)Marital status
(C)Numerical Aptitude   (D)Professional Attitude

17. In the word "RESEARCH" R stands for:

(A)Reasoning   (B)Rational way of thinking
(C)Research for truth   (D)Reward

18. In the word "RESEARCH" E stands for:

(A)Exactness   (B)Emprical
(C)Effect   (D)Effective

19. In the word "RESEARCH" A stands for:

(A)Actual finding   (B)Annotation
(C)Awareness   (D)Analysis

20. "Basic Research" also refers to as:

(A)Fundamental Research   (B)Applied Research
(C)Experimental Research   (D)Historical Research

21. Ranganathan's spiral scientific method, comprises of:

(A)Types of laws
(B)Types of activity
(C)Cardinal stages in the cycle
(D)All of the above

22. In the Ranganathan's spiral of scientific method, "Quadrant-I" lies
    between?

(A)Nadir & Ascendent   (B)Ascendent & Zenith
(C)Zenith & Descendent   (D)Descendent & Nadir

23. The attributes of a "Research Design" consist of:

(A)Objectivity   (B)Reliability
(C)Validity   (D)All of the above

24. "Research Design" is a:

(A)Plan   (B)Structure
(C)Strategy   (D)All of the above

25. "Deliberate wrong information" is a 'disadvantage' of which kind of Research?

(A)Historical Research (B)Random Sampling
(C)Survey Research (D)Experimental Research

26. "Questionnaire" is a tool of:

(A)Sampling   (B)Survey Research
(C)Experimental Research   (D)Historical Research

27. The statement "Sun will rise from the east tomorrow" is a kind of which type of Reasoning?

(A)Deductive Reasoning   (B)Inductive Reasoning
(C)Imprical Reasoning   (D)Random Reasoning

28. When a population under study is very large, which kind of technique will be used?

(A)Sampling   (B)Random
(C)Questionnaire   (D)Experimental

29. Which among the following is a "Repetitive Method" of Research?

(A)Random method   (B)Survey method
(C)Sampling method   (D)Experimental method

30. Which among the following are the types of Research?

(A)Action Research   (B)Applied Research
(C)Basic Research   (D)All of the above

31. Which among the following are the "Approaches to Research"?

(A)Diagnostic Research   (B)Descriptive Research
(C)Social Research   (D)All of the above

32. Discovery of "X-rays & Microwave" is a type of?

(A)Experimental Research   (B)Accidental Research
(C)Survey Research   (D)Historical Research

33. Which type of sampling technique will be used for "Heterogeneous Population"?

(A)Stratified Random Sampling
(B)Systematic Random Sampling
(C)Simple Random Sampling
(D)Multi-stage Sampling

34. When the population is divided into groups on the basis of "Sex, Education, Religion and Income etc." is known as:

(A)Systematic Sampling   (B)Quota Sampling
(C)Snowball Sampling   (D)Judgment Sampling

35. Which among the following are the "Measures of Central Tendency"?

(A)Mean   (B)Median
(C)Mode   (D)All of the above

36. Which among the following are the "Measures of Dispersion"?

(A)Range   (B)Variance
(C)Standard Deviation   (D)All of the above

37. Which among the following are "Statistical Software Packages" for data analysis?

(A)SPSS   (B)Microsoft-Excel
(C)Both of the above   (D)Non of the above

38. "Open-ended and Close-ended" are the types of which "Research Tool"?

(A)Questionnaire   (B)Report
(C)Statistical analysis   (D)Observation

39. Among the following, which "Method of Research" is a "Deep Intensive Study of a Particular Social Unit"?

(A)Theoretical Study   (B)Case Study
(C)Practical Study   (D)Experimental Study

40. Which among the following are the characteristics of Case Study method of Research?

(A)Deep, diagnostic and detailed study
(B)Qualitative analysis
(C)Comprehensive study
(D)All of the above

41. Which among the following can be a source of data for Case Study method of Research?

(A)Observation   (B)Interview
(C)Personal documents   (D)All of the above

42. A research problem can be selected on the basis of:

(A)Dissatisfaction   (B)Discussion
(C)Literature   (D)All of the above

43. A Hypothesis is a:

(A)An assumed solution to the research problem

(B)An intelligent guess to the research problem
(C)A tentative solution to the research problem
(D)All of the above

44. A Hypothesis can be made on the basis of:

(A)Creativity & Knowledge
(B)Experience & Intellect
(C)Analogies
(D)All of the above

45. Directional & Non-Directional are the types of:

(A)Hypothesis   (B)Survey reports
(C)Questionnaire   (D)Observation

46. "Directional Hypothesis" is also known as:

(A)Null Hypothesis   (B)Structured Hypothesis
(C)Declarative Hypothesis   (D)Un-structured Hypothesis

47. The Hypothesis which challenges the assertion of a 'Declarative
    Hypothesis' is known as:

(A)Null Hypothesis   (B)Research Hypothesis
(C)Non-Declarative Hypothesis (D)Non of the above

48. "Null Hypothesis" is also known as:
(A)Statistic Hypothesis   (B)Testing Hypothesis
(C)Declarative Hypothesis   (D)Non of the above

49. Which among the following are the examples of "Probability
    Sampling"?
(A)Simple Random Sampling   (B)Systematic Sampling
(C)Stratified Sampling   (D)All of the above

50. Which among the following are the examples of "Non-Probability
    Sampling"?
(A)Incidental Sampling   (B)Purposive Sampling
(C)Quota sampling   (D)All of the above

Answers

1(A)   2(D)   3(C)   4(D)   5(C)   6(C)   7(C)   8(D)   9(B)

10(A)   11(B)   12(B)   13(D)   14(D)   15(C)   16(D)   17(B)   18(A)

19(D)   20(A)   21(D)   22(A)   23(D)   24(D)   25(C)   26(B)   27(B)

28(A)   29(D)   30(D)   31(D)   32(B)   33(A)   34(B)   35(D)   36(D)

37(C)   38(A)   39(B)   40(D)   41(D)   42(D)   43(D)   44(D)   45(A)

46(C)   47(A)   48(B)   49(D)   50(D)

Assertion & Reason in Library & Information Science

1. **Assertion(A)**: Research results lead to propound new laws, theories & principles.

   Reason(R): Laws, principles & theories are the result of scientific research.

Codes:
(A) Both (A) and (R) is true
(B) (A) is false and (R) is true
(C) (A) is true and (R) is false
(D) Both (A) and (R) is true but (A) is not a correct explanation.

2. **Assertion(A)**: Like other scientists, the social scientists can obtain relevant information by conducting experiments, interviewing people, observing people and reviewing relevant literature.

   Reason(R): Social scientist cannot be as rigorous as can be of natural scientists.

Codes:
(A) Both (A) and (R) is true but (R) is not a correct explanation
(B) Both (A) and (R) is true
(C) Both (A) and (R) is false
(D) (A) is true but (R) is false

3. **Assertion(A)**: Skillful use of research procedures is an art, their appropriate application is research.

   Reason(R): Systematically conducted research leads to generalization.

Codes:
(A) (A) is true but (R) is false
(B) Both (A) and (R) is true but (A) is not a correct explanation
(C) Both (A) and (R) is true
(D) (A) is false but (R) is true

4. **Assertion(A)**: Hypothesis is essential in all types of research.

   Reason(R): Objectives can fulfill the purpose of hypothesis.

Codes:
(A)(A) is false but (R) is true   (B)Both (A) and (R) is true
(C)(A) is true but (R) is false   (D)Both (A) and (R) is false

5. **Assertion(A)**: Library Science has been called science because it has good application of scientific tools & techniques as is applicable in natural science & physical science.

   Reason(R): Experimental method of research has good scope in library science.

Codes:
(A)(A) is true but (R) is false
(B)(A) is false but (R) is true
(C)Both (A) and (R) is true
(D)Both (A) and (R) is true but (R) is not a correct explanation

6. **Assertion(A)**: Present day libraries need to develop social networking tools for their library websites.

   Reason(R): It helps to reach out the patrons where they live & provide service at the point of need.

Codes:
(A)Both (A) and (R) is true
(B)(A) is true but (R) is false
(C)(A) is false but (R) is true
(D)Both (A) and (R) is true but (R) is not a correct explanation

7. **Assertion(A)**: In colon classification (CC), '2' represents mother country & '44' represents India. A library in India can either use '2' OR '44' for India, but the rules allow for choice.

   Reason(R): The above case is a violation of canon of homonyms.

Codes:
(A)Both (A) and (R) is true and (R) is a correct explanation
(B)(A) is false but (R) is true
(C)Both (A) and (R) is true and (R) is not a correct explanation
(D)(A) is true but (R) is false

8. **Assertion(A)**: In library classification, an empty digit helps in interpolation between two consecutive ordinal numbers.

   Reason(R): An empty digit is a digit with ordinal value but no semantic value.

Codes:
(A)(A) is true but (R) is false
(B)Both (A) and (R) is true and (R) is not the correct explanation
(C)Both (A) and (R) is true and (R) is the correct explanation
(D)(A) is false but (R) is true

9. **Assertion(A)**: Migration is the primary strategy used by most of the organizations for digital archiving.

   Reason(R): Migration preserves the physical presence, content, functionality & context of the digital object.

Codes:
(A)Both (A) and (R) is true and (R) is the correct explanation
(B)Both (A) and (R) is true and (R) is not the correct explanation
(C)(A) is false but (R) is true
(D)(A) is true but (R) is false

10. **Assertion(A)**: Making information available using GSDL is effective than just putting it on the web.

    Reason(R): The information available in digital form can be archived.
Codes:
(A)Both (A) and (R) is true and (R) is the correct explanation
(B)Both (A) and (R) is true and (R) is not the correct explanation
(C)(A) is true but (R) is false
(D)(A) is false but (R) is true

11. **Assertion(A)**: In a particular study we may reject the alternative hypothesis.

Reason(R): In the same study the null hypothesis is not rejected.

Codes:
(A)Both (A) and (R) is true and (R) is the correct explanation of (A)
(B)(A) is true but (R) is false
(C)(A) is false but (R) is true
(D)Both (A) and (R) is true and (R) is not the correct explanation of (A)

12. **Assertion(A)**: To increase the specificity we need to accept the long notations.

Reason(R): An important quality of notation is brevity.

Codes:
(A)Both (A) and (R) is true and (R) is not the correct explanation of (A)
(B)(A) is true but (R) is false
(C)(A) is false but (R) is true
(D)Both (A) and (R) is true and (R) is the correct explanation of (A)

13. **Assertion(A)**: Netiquette mandates that you do your best to act within the laws of cyberspace and society.

Reason(R): Failing to respect other people's privacy is bad Netiquette.

Codes:
(A)Both (A) and (R) are false   (B)Both (A) and (R) are true
(C)(A) is true but (R) is false   (D)(A) is false but (R) is true

14. **Assertion(A)**: Modern Integrated Library Management Software offer user friendly Graphical User Interfaces (GUI) on the web.

Reason(R): Almost every module of modern Integrated Library Management Software is accessible through the internet.

Codes:
(A)Both (A) and (R) are correct   (B)(A) is correct but (R) is wrong
(C)Both (A) and (R) are wrong   (D)(A) is wrong but (R) is correct

15. **Assertion(A)**: Open Systems Interconnection allows connectivity of ICT components.

   Reason(R): Network Printer goes slowly if it is OSI compatible.

Codes:
(A)Both (A) and (R) are true   (B)Both (A) and (R) are false
(C)(A) is false but (R) is true   (D)(A) is true but (R) is false

16. **Assertion(A)**: Many libraries have no written collection development policy and yet have sound collection.

   Reason(R): Demand driven collection plays a strong role in having a sound collection.

Codes:
(A)(A) is true, but (R) is false   (B)(A) is false, but (R) is true
(C)Both (A) and (R) are true   (D)Both (A) and (R) are false

17. **Assertion(A)**: Browne charging system is simple and less time consuming.

   Reason(R): There is permanent issue record available.

Codes:
(A)(A) is false but (R) is true   (B)(A) is true but (R) is false
(C)Both (A) and (R) are true   (D)Both (A) and (R) are false

18. **Assertion(A)**: Collection of audio materials is less used in Academic Libraries.

   Reason(R): People consider these materials intellectually less sound and fit only for recreation purpose.
Codes:
(A)(A) is false but (R) is true
(B)(A) is true but (R) is false

(C)(A) is true and (R) is partially true
(D)Both (A) and (R) are false

19. **Assertion(A)**: Introduction of TQM in libraries is not possible.

   Reason(R): It requires open, cooperative culture and employees responsiveness for customer satisfaction.

Codes:
(A)Both (A) and (R) are true   (B)(A) is true but (R) is false
(C)(A) is false but (R) is true   (D)Both (A) and (R) are false

20. **Assertion(A)**: An indexing language is an artificial language and it uses controlled vocabulary.

   Reason(R): Controlled vocabulary provides relation between and among terms.

Codes:
(A)Both (A) and (R) are true   (B)(A) is true but (R) is false
(C)(A) is false but (R) is true   (D)Both (A) and (R) are false

21. **Assertion(A)**: Marketing of Information products is the need of the day.

Reason(R): Information is a resource which consumes lot of time and money.

Codes:
(A)(A) is true but (R) is false   (B)(A) is false but (R) is true
(C)Both (A) and (R) are true   (D)Both (A) and (R) are false

22. **Assertion(A)**: Colon classification is an enumerative classification scheme.

   Reason(R): Colon classification has adopted analytico-synthetic approach for the construction of class number.

Codes:
(A)(A) is false but (R) is true   (B)(A) is true but (R) is false

(C)Both (A) and (R) are true   (D)Both (A) and (R) are false

23. **Assertion(A)**: INFLIBNET provides document delivery service to all types of libraries in India.

    Reason(R): Modern technologies made it possible for electronic transmission of required documents.

Codes:
(A)Both (A) and (R) are correct
(B)(A) is wrong but (R) is correct
(C)Both (A) and (R) are wrong
(D)(A) is correct and (R) is wrong

24. **Assertion(A)**: LIS Education in India achieved a landmark of 100 years but quality is compromised.

    Reason(R): Unplanned proliferation of LIS schools and open learning programmes.

Codes:
(A)Both (A) and (R) are true   (B)Both (A) are (R) are false
(C)(A) is false (R) is true   (D)(A) is true (R) is false

25. **Assertion(A)**: LIS education is not uniform throughout India.

    Reason(R): Adoption of UGC model syllabus is not mandatory, Local LIS requirements varies.

Codes:
(A)(A) is true but (R) is false   (B)(A) is false but (R) is true
(C)Both (A) and (R) are true   (D)Both (A) and (R) are false

26. **Assertion(A)**: There is need for Library Legislation in all States of India.

    Reason(R): To make Public Library System independent and without political influence.

Codes:

(A) Both (A) and (R) are true   (B)(A) is true, but (R) is false
(C) Both (A) and (R) are false   (D)(A) is false, but (R) is true

27. **Assertion(A)**: Though information is considered as a commodity, Libraries are not sound in finances.

Reason(R): All types of Libraries have failed in promoting information as a commodity.

Codes:

(A)(A) is true but (R) is false   (B)(A) is false but (R) is true
(C) Both (A) and (R) are true   (D)Both (A) and (R) are false

28. **Assertion(A)**: Users can have access to large number of e-journals.

Reason(R): Users are not aware of using e-journals.

Codes:

(A)(A) is true but (R) is false
(B) Both (A) and (R) are true but (R) is not the correct explanation of (A)
(C)(A) is false (R) is true
(D) Both (A) and (R) are true and (R) is the correct explanation of (A)

29. **Assertion(A)**: Book selection must be done judiciously.

Reason(R): Resource sharing is the need of the hour.

Codes:

(A) Both (A) and (R) are true, but (R) is not the correct statement of (A)
(B)(A) is false but (R) is true
(C)(A) is true but (R) is false
(D) Both (A) and (R) are false

30. **Assertion(A)**: Primary sources provide most authentic information for research.

Reason(R): Primary sources are highly unorganised.

Codes:
(A)(A) is false but (R) is true
(B)(A) is true but (R) is false
(C)Both (A) and (R) are correct and (R) is the correct explanation of (A)
(D)Both(A)and(R)are correct but(R)is not the correct explanation of (A)

31. **Assertion(A)**: Abstracting services facilitate literature review.

   Reason(R): Literature review summarises major findings of various
                 studies.

Codes:
(A)(A) is true but (R) is false   (B)(A) is false but (R) is true
(C)Both (A) and (R) are true   (D)Both (A) and (R) are false

32. **Assertion(A)**: "Name Authority File" should be used in a library.

   Reason(R): All works of an author should be collocated.

Codes:
(A)(A) is true but (R) is false
(B)Both (A) and (R) true and (R) is the correct explanation of (A)
(C)(A) is false but (R) is true
(D)Both (A) and (R) are false

33. **Assertion(A)**: Classification plays a significant role in online
                 retrieval.

   Reason(R): Classification played an important role in manual
                 system.

Codes:
(A)(A) is true but (R) is false   (B)Both (A) and (R) are false
(C)Both (A) and (R) are true   (D)(A) is false but (R) is true

34. **Assertion(A)**: If changes cannot be adapted to its framework, the
                 organisational equilibrium will be imbalanced.

   Reason(R): Organisation works in an environment which is marked
                 by dynamic characteristics.

Codes:
(A)(A) is true but (R) is false   (B)(A) is false but (R) is true
(C)Both (A) and (R) are true   (D)Both (A) and (R) are false

35. **Assertion(A)**: There is need to continuous evaluation and appreciation of value of libraries.

Reason(R): There is economic pressure on public budget.

Codes:
(A)Both (A) and (R) are true   (B)Both (A) and (R) are false
(C)(A) is true but (R) is false   (D)(A) is false but (R) is true

36. **Assertion(A)**: System analysis identifies the flow of work.

Reason(R): System analysis is not necessary if the library is automated.

Codes:
(A)(A) is false but (R) is true   (B)(A) is true but (R) is false
(C)Both (A) and (R) are false   (D)Both (A) and (R) are true

37. **Assertion(A)**: Internet can replace libraries.

Reason(R): Google searches will satisfy the maximum user's needs.

Codes:
(A)Both (A) and (R) are true   (B)Both (A) and (R) are false
(C)(A) is true but (R) is false   (D)(A) is false but (R) is true

38. **Assertion(A)**: Federated search technique is an integral component of an information portal.

Reason(R): 'Content Index' contains content that is finding by the search server.

Codes:
(A)Both (A) and (R) are true   (B)Both (A) and (R) are false
(C)(A) is true but (R) is false   (D)(A) is false but (R) is true

39. **Assertion(A)**: A combination of hypertext and Hypermedia contains text, images, sounds and other information.

Reason(R): Hypermedia information is represented in a linear fashion.

Codes:
(A)(A) is true and (R) is false   (B)Both (A) and (R) are true
(C)(A) is false and (R) is true   (D)Both (A) & (R) are false

40. **Assertion(A)**: Book selection should be done judiciously.

Reason(R): A library should acquire important and latest book selection tools.

Codes:
(A)(A) is true but (R) is false
(B)(A) is false but (R) is true
(C)Both (A) & (R) are true but (R) is not the correct explanation of (A)
(D)Both (A) & (R) are true and (R) is the correct explanation of (A)

41. **Assertion(A)**: TQM promotes the way in which a library is organised and perform its ICT functions.

Reason(R): TQM is seen as a hindrance to library and information services.

Codes:
(A)Both (A) and (R) are true   (B)Both (A) and (R) are false
(C)(A) is false and (R) is true   (D)(A) is true and (R) is false

42. **Assertion(A)**: The array of classes 11, 12, 13 and the array of classes 31, 32, 33 are said to be collateral arrays.

Reason(R): They are derived from the original universe 'O'.

Codes:
(A)(A) is false (R) is true   (B)(A) is true (R) is false
(C)Both (A) & (R) are true   (D)Both (A) & (R) are false

43. **Assertion(A)**: RDF supports the use and exchange of metadata on the web.

Reason(R): Bibliographic standards are the means to create and disseminate secondary information.

Codes:
(A)(A) is true (R) is false   (B)(A) is false (R) is true
(C)Both (A) & (R) are correct   (D)Both (A) & (R) are false

44. **Assertion(A)**: Informative abstracts provide a concise summary of the subject content of an artide.

Reason(R): These are title-oriented than finding-oriented.

Codes:
(A)Both (A) and (R) are true   (B)(A) is true but (R) is false
(C)(A) is false but (R) is true   (D)Both (A) and (R) are false

45. **Assertion(A)**: E-publications have added enormous quantity of literature but adversely affected the quality of literature.

Reason(R): Present decade has accepted E-publication as channels of fast communication.

Codes:
(A)(A) is true (R) is false
(B)(A) is false but (R) is correct
(C)Both (A) & (R) are false
(D)Both (A) & (R) are true

46. **Assertion(A)**: Encydopaedias are not relevant for finding geographically information.

Reason(R): Encyclopaedias are the substitute for all categories of reference sources.

Codes:
(A)(A) is false but (R) is true   (B)Both (A) and (R) are true

(C)Both (A) and (R) are false   (D)(A) is true but (R) is false

47. **Assertion(A)**: LIS profession is not considered at par with medical and legal professions.

   Reason(R): There is no constitutional body for LIS profession like Medical Council of India (MCI) and Bar Council of India (BCI).

Codes:

(A)Both (A) and (R) are true   (B)Both (A) and (R) are false
(C)(A) is true but (R) is false   (D)(A) is false but (R) is true

48. **Assertion(A)**: Dr.S.R.Ranganathan has been called 'Father of Library and Information Science' in India.

   Reason(R): Library Science education in India was started by Dr.S.R. Ranganathan.

Codes:

(A)(A) is false but (R) is true   (B)(A) is true but (R) is false
(C)Both (A) and (R) are true   (D)Both (A) and (R) are false

49. **Assertion(A)**: The exclusive rights conferred by Intellectual property rights can generally be transferred/ licensed to third parties.

   Reason(R): The creators want to make monetary benefits out of their intellectual product.

Codes:

(A)(A) is true but (R) is false
(B)(A) is false but (R) is true
(C)Both (A) & (R) are true
(D)Both (A) & (R) are false

50. **Assertion(A)**: Machine translation is not a fully dependable service.

   Reason(R): The semantics of languages are not fully encoded in algorithms.

Codes:

(A)(A) is true but (R) is false
(B)Both (A) & (R) are true
(C)(A) is false but (R) is true
(D)Both (A) & (R) is false

UNIT-VIII
Answers

1(C) 2(B) 3(C) 4(A) 5(D) 6(A) 7(A) 8(B) 9(A)

10(B) 11(A) 12(A) 13(B) 14(A) 15(D) 16(C) 17(B) 18(C)

19(C) 20(A) 21(C) 22(A) 23(B) 24(A) 25(C) 26(B) 27(A)

28(B) 29(A) 30(D) 31(C) 32(B) 33(D) 34(C) 35(A) 36(B)

37(B) 38(A) 39(A) 40(C) 41(D) 42(B) 43(C) 44(B) 45(D)

46(A) 47(A) 48(B) 49(C) 50(A)

END